Thoughts For The Soul

A COLLECTION OF INSPIRED WRITINGS

by David **Jezierski**

Printed by
Kerrin Graphics & Printing, Inc.
42 West Dudley Road
Dudley, Massachusetts 01571

Cover Design: Ken Vaudrain

©2020 David Jezierski

Acknowledgments

I would like to thank *Linda Adams, Julie Geary, Father Joseph Marcotte and Anita Compagnone* who took the time to help proofread and recommend edits to my manuscript. I would also like to thank *Adam and Meagan Cannon, Charlie and Jane Gauvin, Julie Geary, Jesse Jezierski, Lisa Jezierski, Michael Kane, David Podbieslki and Patty Podbielski* who supported me financially in the production of this book.

A Personal Note From the Author

Dear friends,

After receiving interior promptings, which I call the "interior communications," I was led to a life-changing, powerful conversion. I was an adult living in a world of sinfulness around me and within me. In my conversion I was awakened from the slumber of darkness in my world of spiritual blindness. Now a child of God's light, I would begin my journey in an unfamiliar world of which I knew little about. In this new world, I journey from childhood to an adult in the spirit using the avenues that God would provide. In the first half of my journey, my understanding of God came through certain individuals whom God put in my path. They tried to assist me as best as they could in getting me closer to God and moving me away from my sinfulness. I eventually became inflated with spiritual pride, walking in a different kind of blindness. I was growing spiritually in leaps and bounds, as one spiritual director put it. But no matter what I was taught I still felt as if I didn't really know God at all. I was still struggling with certain sins, and yet I felt the joy of the Lord in me often. I was at a place, unable to move forward towards a deeper intimacy with God. I knew there was more—and wanted more—and was wondering how I would get there and who would take me. God searched my heart, saw my desires and began speaking to me the interior messages necessary for me to grow in union with Him. The writings of the messages start off in simplicity because of my immaturity in the spirit and my lack of understanding of my sinfulness. The first writings were mostly received during the hours when I was awake; because of my immaturity and my inability to submit my will to His. I knew very little of mortification or of sacrificing myself, which would have made it impossible for me to get out of bed in the early morning to write. God, being the teacher, understood my weaknesses and slowly and gently helped me to see myself through the interior writings. The writings begin in the darkness of my world because of my sinfulness. It is not that I lived in the world of darkness, but because darkness remained within me because of sin. It's my heart crying out—wanting to be free from my sinfulness—as God continues to help me understand my sinfulness and my selfishness through the writings. The writings begin with God's justice which was necessary for my spiritual growth in Him. As the writings continue, He will, at times, reveal His mercy and love in them so that I do not abuse His mercy and abandon His justice. The writings then focus on the spiritual battleground, which we all are on, and the preparation necessary for this battle. As I continue to shed my sinfulness and self-love and grow in virtues, the writings changed to a metaphorical language with poetry inflaming my heart with the beautiful language of God. The last writing, "The Heart of God," confirms the love of God and the sacrifices given to the human race through that love and gives us hope that His heart can flourish in us if we let Him work through us. I pray that, through the writings, you do not misunderstand the intentions of them. They were spoken to me so that I could find God in a deeper and more meaningful relationship with Him through an avenue of sacrificial love and growing in virtues. The ultimate goal is union with God. It is not an easy one, but not an impossible one. How you think, along with the desires of your heart, is where your journey will begin. How far you can go is up to you. How much you are willing to give up of yourself to live in a more perfect love is up to you. God will draw you to Himself if you let Him, only if you let Him.

David

 Inviting the Holy Spirit

Come Holy Spirit, come.
Come Holy Spirit, come.
Open our minds Holy Spirit, open our minds.
Open our hearts Holy Spirit, open our hearts.
Comfort us Holy Spirit, comfort us.
Purify our souls Holy Spirit, purify our souls.
Purify our bodies Holy Spirit, purify our bodies.
Heal our brokenness Holy Spirit, heal our brokenness.
Heal our physical ailments Holy Spirit, heal our physical ailments.
Bring us hope Holy Spirit in your healing power, bring us hope.
We are broken Holy Spirit, we are broken.
We believe in your healing power Holy Spirit, we believe.
Come Holy Spirit, come.
Come Holy Spirit, come.
Our hearts are open Holy Spirit, our hearts are open.
Our minds are open Holy Spirit, our minds are open.
Our souls are open Holy Spirit, our souls are open.
We love You Jesus, we love You.
We need You Jesus, we need You.
Have mercy on us Jesus, have mercy on us.
Forgive us Jesus, forgive us.
Heavenly Father have mercy on us, Heavenly Father have mercy on us.
Blessed Mother pray for us, Blessed Mother pray for us.
Come Holy Spirit, come.
Come Holy Spirit, come.
Let us feel Your presence Holy Spirit, let us feel Your presence.
We need You Holy Spirit, we need You.
We thank You Holy Spirit, we thank You.
We love You Holy Spirit, we love You.
Come Holy Spirit, come.
Come Holy Spirit, come.

CONTENTS

Miscellaneous Thoughts	1
The Within	6
The Lost	7
My Last Day Prayer	8
Alone	9
Christ Crucified	10
Shadows of the Soul	11
Mother	12
Gratitude	13
The Cup of Worldliness	14
I Am Who Am	15
Mommy	16
The Battle Within	17
Fallen Houses	18
Love	19
Hope	20
The Kingdom	21
Mercy	22
The Wall	23
Christian	24
Deceiver	25
The Mirror and Glass	26
Table of Unforgiveness	27
Frail	28
Father	29
The Cross	30
Darkness	31
Fading Away	32
Purge	33
Worlds Apart	34
Darkness and Light	35
Letting Go	36
Surrender	37
Death	38
Holding On	39
Time	40
Search My Heart	41
My Eyes	42
Pure of Heart	43
Walk With Me	44
Obstacles	45
The Journey	46
Castles	47
Measurement of Love	48
Our Hearts	49
Save Me	50
Arena	51
The Visitor	52
Breath of Life	53
Armored	54

The Mountain	55
Final Preparation	56
Prideful	57
Table of Knights	58
Friendship	59
The Walk	60
Baptism	61
Penance	62
Communion	63
Confirmation	64
Marriage	65
Behold	66
The Battlefield	67
The Spirits	68
The Unending Battle	69
The Broken Covenant	70
Sin	71
Fallen Angel	72
Broken Cup	73
Blind	74
Children of Disobedience	75
Struggle	76
False Gods	77
Purgatory	78
Traveling Souls	79
Desert Storms	80
Dark Nights	81
Perfection	82
Predestination and the Will	83
Rose Scarlet	84
Thoughts	85
Powers of this World	86
Hidden	87
Impure	88
Go Back	89
Murky Waters	90
The Waters of Despair	91
How do I Love You	92
Do You See the Evil	93
True Freedom	94
Trapdoors	95
Descend to Ascend	96
Human Love	97
Crucify the Flesh	98
Heaven	99
Imperfect Lover	100
The Pool	101
The Final Battle	102
Illusions	103
Temptations	104
The Heart of God	105

 Miscellaneous Thoughts

Love has to be purified before it can be glorified.

I could not see inside myself,
the eye to my soul was blind.
I could not know who I was until I became
who I am.
I could not be what I am until God
became part of me.
I cannot be until I let go of me and
unite with you, Lord.
Apart from you, Lord, what could I be?

It has come to my inner understanding that the world, in its evolving thinking, has evolved from the concept that we offend God. That when we sin we offend the only true source of love. Abusing mercy has brought us from the reality that our sins offend Him.

Sin took me from You, oh Lord, but your mercy set me free. Now I walk in the corridors of hope to the possibilities of complete union with You, for grace has given me the understanding and the freedom to accomplish what only the soul can do in-flight.

The soul's ability to understand itself, and truly see inside itself, may come to this. That the soul must have the capacity to understand the spiritual life, and see within so that the soul can try to see past the wall of deception in the present mode of his or her spirit. This blindness only allows a soul a limited understanding of the state the soul is in.

I could not know my love for my Lord unless I knew my weaknesses, for in my weakness I found my strength, not by myself but in the one who showed me.

The kingdom is able to be found for those who search for it. How can anything be found if one does not know what they are searching for and do not seek to find it?

Evil cannot enter through the door of my soul unless I open it to the unwelcome guest. Once in, he will steal the things that are good and replace them with false things.

The soul, in its sorrow here upon this earth, has no home here, so it searches to the heavens. God so chose that soul to suffer so. The soul must now see its imperfections and weaknesses and its helplessness.

When a man is strong he relies on his own strength. But when he is made weak he no longer relies on his own strength so he searches. Let his search bring him to God, for in God's will he will find great strength and love.

Time is an exchange, time is a gift, never the same given to an individual for we take time and use it as we will, only to give an account of it later, never truly the owner, only the borrower.

God will open a door for you, but you must decide if you will walk in with complete trust in God, or will you remain standing outside the door in fear.

You will find silence a great place, no gossip, no slander, only peace.

Faith is not for the foolish or the blind, it is for the believer whose heart and mind is open.

Love is only as strong as one's ability to sacrifice.

I embraced the cross not knowing it had so much love pouring from it.

The hardest cross you can bear is not the crosses I give you, but the ones you put upon yourself.

Sometimes it is difficult to pray in a storm, but not impossible.

Love is beautiful in the perfection of itself, perfect love.

Tears of joy fall to the ground, tears of suffering rise to the heavens.

A word alone is just a word, a group of words form a sentence, then a paragraph, then a page, then a book. So it is in your journey, a cross starts the relationship, then many crosses build it. Then it can be forged in the will of God reaching perfection in Him.

We reward what should be punished, and we punish what should be rewarded.

The interior sees beyond the imagery of the deception to the depths of the soul where the truth is hidden.

That which is created sacred is beautiful in its sacredness.

Perception is not truth, and can be deceiving to a soul in sin.

Jesus said "yes" to His Father, Mary said "yes" to God, the Saints said "yes" to Jesus. By saying "yes," they all received great suffering uniting their suffering as one, as it will be for those who say "yes, Lord."

To hear only one person's viewpoint may lead to blindness. For the other person's viewpoint may contain the truth.

The flesh pulls at us drawing every breath it can in hopes of clinging to this world. But the spirit, in the crucified state, wants to be free of the flesh through crucifixion.

A person cannot be truly happy until he or she finds and lives in the truth.

Pride and humility are like oil and water, you have to scoop out the pride before you can get to the humility.

Imagery disappears when it faces reality.

The sky was blue then turned dark by the words of the unknowing.

I looked with the eyes of hope and forgiveness wondering if I am blind and stupid. Can the rainbow have a happy ending or is it just a dream for fools?

Deception is its strongest when hidden in the sands of false images that is believed to be true.

Perception: How another one perceives you is not how you perceive yourself. We are all somewhat blinded to ourselves.

My heart was forged in the stone of this world. You, oh Lord, took my stony heart and turned it into flesh. The love of You, Lord, dwells in me giving new life to the risen me in You.

The truth can heal or destroy that which contains imperfection or deception.

Faith is a measurement of that which cannot be seen or held.

We look in the direction we think we should be going, but God is pointing us in the direction that we are to go, and we do not even see Him.

Do not let the weight of the world bring you down. A good soul lives to ascend towards the heavenly promise.

Death of a child is never easy, and consoling the ones left behind may be even harder, but God is the only one who has the answers to life's difficult unknown questions. Death is life in a new place for those who believe, and hope gives us life through death.

Addictions

I stood in front of the door, and there was a word written upon it, so I walked towards the door to read it. The name upon the door was addiction. I was curious so I opened the door and walked in. Then the hand of addiction reached out and pulled me in. It would not let me go, I begged it for mercy. It said to me you should never have opened the door, now you are my slave. We must always be careful before we open the door to anything, for we may never get free from the grip of addiction.

Inward

I thought to myself, who am I? So I looked inward for I could not see myself in the mirror. So I looked within. I found myself deep within. I was a prisoner to myself. Inside my soul was the light and darkness of myself, they battled inside me. At times, the darkness covered the light. Then there were times the light was so bright I could not see the darkness. Then I heard the voices of darkness and light, they spoke words to my soul, and my soul cried out, for it wanted the darkness to go away, for the darkness caused it so much pain.

Judgment

It is said, "do not judge." Since judgment comes from within, to what direction do you judge? If you spare judgment, do you spare the soul from damnation? If you must judge, and when you do judge, judge only out of love. In love, judgment is for the well-being of the soul, and not damnation.

The Light

The faith of the saints and the martyrs never lost sight of the truth. The truth was deep within them. As the light of the sun fills the earth so does the light of God fill their soul. How can anyone turn away from that which is so beautiful unless it has not experienced it. If the joys of this world deceive my soul, then I cannot experience the fullness of that light.

Pieces

Let your heart break because of your own weaknesses. Then let your heart break for all the people and their weaknesses. Then let all the pieces fall to the ground. Look at them and tell me what you see. Lord, what should I see? You should see Me.

Direction

When a soul loses focus on God, then it loses direction on that it was to focus. Then the soul opens the doors to temptation, falling from its true focus which would have protected the soul from sin. Deception stops every good thought that could have been and every good emotion that could have been felt. This void of deception exists in lost souls.

The Moment
I do not live in the past, nor do I look to the future, so I live in the present, even on my deathbed, for at the time of my death I will go from the present here to the present day there for time does not exist with God.

Truth
God is truth which all truth must pass through and come from, for no truth can exist without God. For the origin of truth is God. To find God one must find truth. You cannot find God in deception. For God cannot exist outside of the truth. There is only one truth; it cannot be altered from its origin. Deception moves us away from that origin. It separates us and distances us also. When I move towards what is true, I find what is true, I find God.

Conversion
God is light, the soul in sin dwells in darkness. To understand how the soul gets to darkness you need to form an understanding. When we sin, it is as if we took a piece of glass and smudged it, and we put the piece of glass between God and ourselves. Every time we sin we take a new piece of glass and smudge it and put the new piece of glass between God and ourselves. Over time there are so many pieces of glass between God and ourselves that God's light, over time, cannot pierce the pieces of glass between God and us. In God's mercy he takes his hand and smashes all the glass, and His light pierces our soul. The soul now begins its journey towards God with a clearer vision. For what once separated the soul from God has been removed. And the light of truth enters a soul. And the soul continues in search of the light.

Solitude
I have found the place of solitude; it is found in the heartbreak and suffering in our life. There you will see everything for what it really is.

Interior Life
God can bring you to a place within a place, a home within a house, and a room within a room. This is the interior life.

Their World
We cannot enter the world of worldly thought and emotion, for if we do we become part of it. The spirit of God will not enter and will remain outside waiting for us, for when we are in the flesh we fall to the same fate.

Children
Enjoy the flowers while they are here, tend their needs as best you can, water them in hopes that they will grow, remember the time will come when the flower petals will fall to the earth. They shall not return to the flower as they once were attached to.

 The Within

Oh Lord, I thought I knew You but I was wrong.
All these years I wandered never knowing.
I never really searched for You, but You were there.
I was surrounded by everything You created,
and I never saw You anywhere.
You surrounded me, and You were within me.
It took so long to find You,
and when I found You, deep within my soul,
I did not know how to love You.
You were very patient with me—
though I deserved nothing, You gave me all.
I was living outside myself,
never looking deep within myself.
You were always there, as You are with everyone.
You let me wander among the world.
You let me lose myself to the world.
You let me experience the emptiness of the world.
You still were deep within me,
You spoke from within me,
and I heard Your voice from within.
You poured Your grace upon me,
You opened the door inside, so I could come in from the outside.
So I left the world that surrounded me
and embraced You inside myself.
I found a new home inside myself with You;
the place where I can be alone with You.
The place no one can enter except You;
a place of silence, a place of peace.
When I go outside myself You are still within me,
and when I return You never close the door on me.
I know You are everywhere, and see everything,
but the best place to find You is within.

 The Lost

I have loved you from the beginning of time, and I always will.
These are the words I spoke to you before you came to be.
Know that I am in heaven always, waiting for you;
know that you can call upon My name at anytime and anywhere.
I was with you inside your mother's womb.
I was with you as a child when you used to pray to Me at night.
You were so innocent, so precious, so uncorrupted.
As you got older, we began to drift apart.
I watched you move away and it broke My heart.
You were searching for the stars, looking for happiness in all the wrong places—
you went in search of your dreams and left Me behind.
I tried to let you know I was there, but you never heard My voice.
You took the empty road, the road of sin, the road of separation.
I never stopped loving you, and I never will.
The sin consumed you, deceived you, and separated you from Me.
You thought you were happy, but the happiness only lasted a little while;
you felt so empty, so alone.
You cried out My name and never waited for a response.
I was there right by your side, but you could not see Me.
Your soul was so full of deception, it would not let Me in.
You closed the door to My face, and I stood outside.
I had so much mercy I wanted to give you, but
you never really sincerely wanted My mercy or My love.
So much I wanted to give you, so much you could receive;
in the end you were so lost, you could not find your way.
Lost and deceived you ended your life, how that saddened Me that day.
You never returned to Me for I waited for you.
You chose to reject My mercy and love for everything else.
I gave you free will and you abused it.
Now you stand before Me, broken, lost, and all alone.
I look in your eyes, I am saddened, heartbroken, wishing it could be different.
By your choices in life, desires of your heart, and your rejection of Me,
it comes to this. It hurts Me so much because we have to say goodbye forever.
I have loved you from the beginning of time, and I always will.

My Last Day Prayer

Lord, thank You for every blessing and every suffering,
for every person You put before me good or bad,
for all the days happy or sad, for always being there.
And if I should wake today, and tomorrow never comes,
let my day bring glory to You, O Lord.

Let the people I see today see Christ in me,
not like in the past, where I failed so many times before.
Let my day be an outpouring of Your love
for so many times I have hurt those You love.
Let my selfish nature remain inside
for so many times I thought of myself.
Let my personal feelings never get in the way of Your will
for so many times I did things my way not Yours.

Let me make no excuses for who I am;
I am a sinner in so much need of Your mercy.
Let me not justify my wrongdoings and shortcomings;
with Your grace help me to overcome them.
Let me be truthful to myself and others,
so I never deceive and lead others astray.

Let me desire what You desire;
it seems that my desires keep You away.
Let me have done all that You wanted me to do,
knowing there is nothing more You wanted me to do.
Lord, if today is my last day on this earth,
let my last words be words loving You.

Amen

 Alone

For those who can truly be alone with God, you will know,
understand, and never return back to the world.
God is the perfect lover of souls, the perfect friend,
the true source of peace, and the completion of life.
Before God came into my life, I walked a road searching.
I thought I had it all, not realizing I had nothing.
I thought I possessed it all, not realizing I possessed nothing.
I always wanted, but never really felt satisfied.
I was continuously searching and never found true peace.
I thought the world had much to offer, but I was wrong!
I fell into worldly addictions without knowing, and it imprisoned my soul.
Soon the light within me was almost gone.
Darkness filled my soul, it left me so alone.
I cried out to the heavens, my only source of hope,
and the hands of God opened full of mercy and compassion.
I began my new journey towards God and His love.
I left the world behind because I felt so incomplete.
As I grew deeper in union with God, the world seemed empty.
I could not find joy in those things that used to possess me.
The Lord tested my love for Him;
it seemed so hard I felt I could not go on.
At times, I could not feel the presence of God within myself
for God was going deeper inside me.
I was feeling empty, alone, with no desire to go back.
I could only go forward to the loving arms of God.
God was waiting for me to search for Him, to love Him,
to desire Him over all things in a perfect relationship.
A relationship uncorrupted without worldly desires,
from all the things that separated me from God.
You can build your kingdom here on this earth.
You can live in a world full of empty promises.
You can pretend you are really happy and continue searching.
Or you could begin your new journey towards God.
In the world alone, you will truly feel alone.
In the alone with God, you still can live in peace.
In the alone (the interior life) you will find God.
The world will always appear to offer you so much,
but only God will leave you feeling complete.

Christ Crucified
the gift of love

There are those who never heard of Jesus.
There are those who have and do not believe.
There are those who have and do not understand.
He left behind the greatest love story ever told.
For God was His father who sent His son.
Jesus came for the lost in the hope they would be found.
Jesus preached the message of His Father's love.
Jesus was also sent to die for the forgiveness of our sins.
Jesus performed many miracles, including raising of the dead
and healing the sick, spiritually and physically.
Jesus came as the ultimate sacrifice for humanity.
In the end, after all Jesus did, they crucified Him.
Did you ever look up at the cross and wonder?
Can you even understand the price paid?
The love it took, the pain endured, the sacrifice made?
What kind of love would suffer so much for so little in return?
For every drop of blood that fell to the ground
not one drop was for Himself, for selfishness never existed in Him.
This is the purest of love that denies itself totally.
Jesus never thought of His own needs, only ours.
So when you look upon that cross,
try to ponder the greatest love that ever existed;
follow the greatest example of love ever seen,
which Jesus showed us upon that cross.
The footsteps laid in the soil of the earth,
the ultimate sacrifice, the price paid in full.
The greatest gift of the perfect love.

(Reflection)

How Your heart must have broken when everyone You loved
turned and walked away from You and left You to die alone.
Only your mother, the apostle John, and a few of Your followers
were with You. The rest hid in fear or just forgot about You.
Most of the people there mocked and cursed You.
Why does such a great sacrifice not pierce our hearts fully?
Why do we give You so little in return?
Why are we too busy to spend more time with You?
Have we forgotten the greatest gift of the perfect love?

Shadows of the Soul

It sees but does not see.
It knows but does not understand.
It loves but loves nothing.
It wants and does not know what it wants.
It lives in a dream and finds no peace.
It searches and never finds.
It exists, not knowing why it exists.
These are the shadows of the soul.
We all want to feel loved,
yet sometimes we find it hard to love.
Do we put ourselves before others?
Do we ever look at ourselves for who we really are?
Does deception keep us from the truth?
Do we really care about the truth?
Deep within all of us exists the truth,
covered by deceptions of false dreams and images.
Shadows that deceive us from a deeper union with God.
All the joys of this world are temporary;
they cling to the flesh like drops of water.
In time they will dry up and disappear.
They form illusions blinding the soul from the truth.
They form a wall of deception deep within us,
creating a way of life pleasing to the flesh,
changing the true call of the soul to be in harmony with God.
Shadows are images or reflections—
but never are truly there, never real,
never genuine, and never to be held.

 Mother

Where does one begin to describe you? For no words can.
Your yes to God changed the future of the whole world.
Your loving heart brought salvation to a world in such need of it,
and the hardships you bore were for the love of God and all humanity.
You would not be just the Mother of one, but the Mother of all.
To those who never knew their mother.
To those who did, but never felt love.
To those who do know their mother and feel loved.
To the whole human race, know this, Mary is Mother of all!
How can words describe the sacrifices you made?
How can we understand the joy you felt carrying the Son of God,
and the crosses you bore for the rejection of your Son Jesus?
For the world rejected God's gift—His Son and yours.
They took your Son Jesus and crucified Him,
and you humbled yourself to the world that took Him from you.
Not one word of hatred or anger ever came from your mouth,
for you loved and forgave the ones who condemned your Son.
You trusted God totally with no terms and no conditions.
You carried the pain of true love and never complained once.
You shared in the joy of Jesus' resurrection,
and when your Son ascended to heaven you remained behind.
You continued the work of your Son until the day of your Assumption.
And from heaven, you continued the work of your Son.
For your Son was, and is, the hope and salvation of this world.
He said He would not return until the end of times.
You continue to appear to this world in such need of your Son.
You have come to us in apparitions and visions.
For you love the world, as God and your Son love the world.
Mary, our Mother, who loves each and every one of us with
a love so powerful that it cannot be described or duplicated.
For no mind could ever understand or conceive this kind of love.
Knowing this, let our thanks, as weak as it is, be some sign of gratitude,
to the Mother who gave all for the love of all.

Amen.

 Gratitude

Gratitude remembers even the smallest of things,
no matter how slight or insignificant the gift seems to be.
It remembers the giver of the gifts as well,
even if the person is just a small part of our life.
True gratitude should remember the giver of life.
Yet it seems at times we forget. Why do we forget?
Does our selfish nature keep us from remembering
to be thankful to God who thinks of us always?
Not just for the gifts He gives us, but because He loves us.
Are we thankful for every moment in our lives?
The laughter, the tears, the joys, and the sorrows.
Whatever it is in our lives You gave to us, Lord.
It is You who formed us through all these things.
It is You because You love us unconditionally.
You brought us into existence.
So let us see and understand this, O Lord.
Allow us to be forever grateful to You,
lover of all souls, to You be the glory forever.
For the days and nights, long or short, You were there.
So much has not been said, so much has been forgotten.
So much to be thankful for and not a word ever spoken.
So many gifts we received, never to be given a thought.
Forgive us for what we take, and have taken for granted.
Sometimes do we think we work hard for things and deserve them?
Without You Lord, how could we ever accomplish anything?
How could we ever love? How could we ever care? How could we ever be?
We know we have forgotten a lot of these things.
Through all the trials and hardships You were there.
Do we really appreciate God? Do we ever give Him a thought?
Who would understand, unless one knew You were forming them.
You are the giver of all these gifts.
May our selfish nature never deny the gratitude that is truly Yours,
and let Your unconditional love never be forgotten.

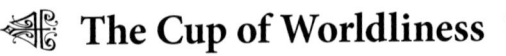 The Cup of Worldliness

We all have, and will continue, to drink of this cup.
For I have drunk too much already.
Every drop is like a poison to my soul.
I wish never to open my mouth and receive another drop.
My veins overflow and I wish it would leave me.
Slowly, with the grace of God, my veins become purer.
My soul desires to drink of a better cup—the cup of life.
How I long for that day when my soul will be purer.
My heart will beat again with the love of God,
freed of worldly desires and selfishness.
My vision will be clearer, and I can behold the truth in its fullness.
My soul in this corrupted state longs to be free,
free of all the things that keep me from my true love.
For worldliness comes in many varieties and tastes—
so appealing to the flesh, so hard to resist.
You, Oh Lord, hold the cup, and are the cup of life.
Let me close my mouth to the cup of worldliness,
and open my mouth only to You, the cup of life.
Take my veins, open them up, let them drain upon this earth.
Empty them totally, so not one drop remains within me.
Pour into me Your cup, the cup of eternal life.
Fill my veins, so I can be made whole.
Let our hearts beat as one and our love flow together.
Let our thoughts unite, let me immerse into Your love.
Imprison me, so the world can never get me.
Lock the door to my soul and throw away the key.
I will wait as long as it will take You to do this.
Continue to form me into what You desire.
Strip me clean, teach me Your ways, and I will find You.
For that day I await the arms of love I will embrace.

 I Am Who Am

For no mind could even begin to understand Me.
For no eyes have ever seen Me, nor could they ever look at Me.
I let them hear My voice and feel My presence.
I allowed them to search for Me when I brought mankind into existence.
And I will allow them to continue their search for Me.
I gave them My commandments. I gave them ways to find Me.
I am, because I always was, and that is beyond human thought.
Who am, because I always will be. I was not created, I am beyond creation.
I exist within My creation. I exist outside of My creation.
I created everything that is, and everything that ever will be.
I created time and space, and everything within it.
I created every living creature and gave it purpose.
I am love in the purest form, if one could ever conceive that.
I am justice, **I am** mercy, **I am** forgiveness, **I am** love.
I created everything out of love with mankind in My thoughts.
I did not create evil. Evil came to be from a thought of the will.
Evil entered paradise, evil deceived man and woman
and man and woman became broken.
I allowed evil to walk the face of the earth because mankind chose to let evil in.
I never stripped mankind of paradise, it is still here waiting for them.
But they must choose which paradise they want—
the paradise I set aside for them which lasts forever,
or a temporary paradise here, which will lead to eternal damnation.
For inside every human being, I have put My spirit which dwells in everyone.
My arms are open, waiting to embrace them if they let themselves go.
I am who am, who will always be, I will never fade away.
But know, your life here is truly temporary, and your choice.
Know your choice will determine where you will spend the rest of your life.
Where do you really want to spend the rest of your life?
You can look to the heavens for Me, but know that **I am** here with you.
You can find Me. I am not far from you, you just have to open your eyes.
Look around you, you will see Me in all My creation.
Listen to My voice, you might hear it in the wind.
Listen to My prophets, through their voices you might come to know Me.
You are My children, will you return to Me? **I am who am**.

 Mommy

The voice of an unborn child:

Hello Mommy, it's me. I know we never had a chance to meet,
so many questions, and I have no answers.
I don't understand why you aborted me, please tell me why.
Mommy, help me to understand, because I don't understand.
You never gave me a chance, why didn't you give me a chance?
Did Daddy want me? How about you? Who didn't want me?
Did you think that I would have been a burden, so you had to let me go?
All I wanted was for you to love me, I would have loved to have been with you.
Mommy, I love you so much, it's hard to forget that day.
All I remember was hearing your heart beat and people talking.
They weren't very nice people, they did mean things to me,
Mommy, didn't you hear me crying for help?
Why didn't you help me Mommy, why didn't you help me?
I was crying in pain and it hurt so bad, I just wanted it to end,
Mommy, why did you let those people hurt me?
I thought you loved me, how could you have done that to me.
I remember I could no longer hear your heart beat,
I could no longer feel the warmth of your body, I felt so cold,
I could no longer hear anyone's voices, I felt so alone,
and then this Beautiful Lady appeared to me.
She seemed like an angel, and said she was my Mother,
she said she had many children, and we are all special to her.
I was no longer afraid or in any pain, I was happy again.
The Beautiful Lady loves me so much, and I love her.
She said for me to forgive you, and she helped me to understand.
Mommy, I forgive you, and I still love you,
I would like to have known you and spent time with you.
I cannot return to you there, but maybe you can come here with me.
The Beautiful Lady said for you to tell Jesus you are really sorry,
to pray always, go to church, and spend time with Jesus.
She said we would be together again for all eternity,
and Mommy, we would be so happy together.
I love you Mommy, I hope someday you will please come home.

The Battle Within

Inside all of us is a battle fought in the interior of ourselves.
This war is not fought with our hands or any part of our bodies,
the battle is against our human nature which includes our sinful nature.
Our will in Christ, against our own will of this world.
The love of God, against our sinful nature which offends God.
The sinful nature keeps us from a deeper intimacy with God.
As oil and water can never mix with each other,
so it is with the sinful nature that is opposite of God, who is pure love.
God loves us unconditionally and gives us free will.
Does our will keep us from not knowing, not understanding,
and not accepting the very things of God and His love?
Are we too weak, too far from Him, to truly know and love Him?
Do we need God's help to remove certain sins that keep us from Him?
Does the sinful nature that dwells within us leave room for God to dwell in us?
Our sinful nature offends God, do we really understand this?
Our sinful nature makes it impossible to feel His presence and His love.
Unless we begin to search inside ourselves to find those things
that keep us from Him, we can never feel the depth of God's love.
There are depths to the sinful nature as well.
For example, the selfish nature—
Do you see love in the selfish nature? Can love dwell there?
How about pride—can you find humility there?
How about hate—can you find forgiveness there?
These are a few examples of the sinful nature which is opposite of God.
The stronger the sinful nature is in us, the further we drift from God's love
making it harder to feel His presence in us and His love for us.
If the sinful nature inside ourselves does not change, the circumstances
cannot change. Our emotions and how we treat others will remain the same.
With God's grace, we can rewrite the sinful nature inside us that is not of God.
God is love, anything opposite to that is not of God,
and if not of God, then it becomes a void within us.
These voids leave us empty and in search of something.
Unless they are filled with the things of God, you will be empty.
Why be empty? Fight the battle within, let God's love prevail.
From the beginning of time, remember what God called us to be.
We were all called to be the true children of God!

Fallen Houses

The Servant:

It saddens my heart that I have to write about fallen houses,
houses intended to bring mankind closer to God, Himself.
Houses fallen from within by the shepherds called to build them.
Prophets of God, fallen to this world, lost and drifted from the truth.
They have given up the things of God for the love of this world—
disillusioned and deceived, walking among the dead,
sacrificing their eternal life for the temporary joys of this world,
building kingdoms and paradises with false hopes and false dreams,
turning the sheep away by their very actions, abandoning God's sheep.
Not all of His shepherds, only some of the shepherds;
they were once shepherds of God, now shepherds of the world.
So now the sheep wander among the lost and confused,
looking to the shepherds for guidance in hope of finding the kingdom.
The shepherds cannot give a gift they do not possess, only what they
do possess. If they are worldly, they will teach the flock to be worldly;
if they are holy, they will teach the flock holiness.
The sheep do not need false hopes and false dreams,
they need guidance and protection from the shepherd.
So the sheep are scattered with nowhere to turn.
They see the shepherd corrupted and seduced by this world.
They keep searching for a shepherd to guide them to Jesus,
praying God will change the shepherd's heart and open his eyes,
waiting for the shepherd to return back to God and embrace His love.
For the houses are fallen and the flocks are scattered.
They justify their wrongdoing in the name of God.
This is not something new, it has happened too many times before!

Our Lord:

Tell the shepherds to open their hearts and minds to the truth,
to pick up their staffs, and return to the flocks to guide them to the gates.
Tell the shepherds that My houses are falling, and to rebuild them.
Tell the shepherds to imitate the life of My Son, to pick up their crosses,
and carry their crosses as Jesus, My Son, has asked them to.
For if those shepherds do not return to Me and My sheep,
they will have this world, and will receive no part of My kingdom.
So many have labored and sacrificed their lives for My houses.
Tell the good shepherds their sacrifices will not be in vain,
that their love for Me and My flock will not go unnoticed.
The gates of Heaven are wide open to the shepherds of My Son Jesus.
Tell the shepherds to bring the flock home with them for all eternity.

 Love

I ask you to embrace your most trusted friend,
for Love will never abandon those who embrace it.
Let Love rise above all things; let nothing come before it.
Let Love open the doors that cannot be opened
and close the doors that should never be opened.
I am not speaking of the world's thinking of what Love is
because it rewrites the truth of Love in a disordered way.
Love is not lustful or sinful; it is not perverted or corrupted.
It is pure, uncorrupted, and does not seek its own interests.
It is not self-seeking, but denies itself totally.
Love finds no joy in pleasing itself for it denies the selfish nature.
It endures hardships and suffering for the love of another.
It embraces the sorrows and the pains of those who suffer around it.
Love is the meaning of life. It is the tree of life with many branches.
Some of these branches are mercy, compassion, forgiveness,
truth, sacrifice, and friendship. You would be wise to embrace them, too.
These branches are almost as strong as the tree itself—
you can count on them; they will never let you down.
Love does not know itself, is not consumed with itself,
finds no satisfaction in itself—only in the joy of others.
Jesus showed us on the cross the true source of Love.
So I encourage you to look at the cross and try to understand.
Love will sacrifice its own life for the love of another.
It will withstand persecution, humiliation, and great pain;
endure suffering of all kinds for the love of others.
Beware of the enemies of Love.
You would be wise to never let them into the door of your heart.
Keep them in the back of your mind, for they will divide Love.
They are pride, jealousy, unforgiveness, selfishness, anger, gluttony, lust,
and the desire for power and wealth leading to the control of another—
any form of self-love that seeks its own interests.
They will only cause suffering between one another.
There is always hope in Love, and Love always offers hope.
You will find joy beyond your wildest dreams when you embrace Love
and Love in return will embrace you and never let you down.
Even if someone else's selfishness should break your heart,
never stop loving.
Love will always prevail, and you will prevail in it.

 Hope

Where does hope begin? Where does hope end?
It begins with God and should end in God.
Everything in the middle is part of the journey.
Sometimes we put our hope in the securities of this world.
Sometimes we put our hope in people.
Sometimes we put our hope in ourselves.
There are no guarantees when we put our hope in these things.
There is always hope through God when hope is understood.
When we put our hope in God and His will, then we can begin to understand.
We can accept what seemed to be hopeless and without meaning.
Although we will not be able to fully understand what God's will is for us,
we can know without a doubt: God knows what is best for us.
Remember the apostles, when they thought Jesus came to this earth
to establish a kingdom here, not knowing Jesus would be crucified.
They put their hope in the living Christ. When they crucified Him,
their spirits were crushed. Only after Jesus' resurrection from the dead,
and with the aid of the Holy Spirit, were the apostles converted.
Their hearts and minds were changed and they repented of their old ways.
They no longer misunderstood the focus of their hope.
Where do you find your hope? Where is the focus of your hope?
For us, hope can be found in repentance.
Through repentance comes the conversion of the soul.
For the soul can begin to unite itself with God.
It is so necessary for this to happen in order to understand hope.
Why do we put so much hope in so many things only to be let down?
Hope is a doorway that opens and closes by our will.
When the doorway is open, we feel the joy of our will.
When the doorway is closed, we feel the pain of our will.
One should never give up hope in anything or anyone.
Hope can open the door to many things—the possibilities are endless.
Try to understand—hope in mankind can only go so far.
Hope in God is endless and true in everything He created.
For if God created mankind and everything in the universe,
then surely He created everything for the love of us.
We hope because we love; because we love there is hope.
God is the purest love. God is the truest and greatest hope we have.
My hope is in my Lord and in His will, though I may not fully understand it.
I will trust in the One who loves me unconditionally.
And in that love for us, to hope in anything else would be futile.

 The Kingdom

Do not store up treasures for yourself upon this earth.
For where your treasures are will be the desires of your heart.
So why do we build our kingdoms here upon this earth?
Why do some desires possess us more than others?
At what price are our kingdoms built?
To those who wish to build kingdoms here upon this earth,
to those who have already built kingdoms here upon this earth,
what will be the spiritual cost?
How many souls will be lost for these temporary joys?
This worldly kingdom is a false illusion that deceives the soul.
There is no greater kingdom than the kingdom of God,
the cross that carried the weight of the world.
For what on this earth can carry that?
Let us not be deceived, for nothing here is truly ours.
We will hold on to the things of this world for a little while,
thinking we own them, and then we have to let them go.
For your kingdom here is truly temporary,
and your kingdom will fall into the hands of others.
Into their hands they will receive empty dreams,
false joys, illusions of hope, and temporary securities.
Jesus is the only treasure one should ever hope to possess.
His kingdom is the only kingdom that lasts forever.
So lay not upon this earth the desires of your heart.
Desire what is above and nothing short of that.
For in the faces of the angels and saints you will see
the joy they receive from union with their true love, God Himself.
There are no false hopes, no false dreams, only the truth.
A kingdom built on truth. Truth alone. Nothing more, nothing less.
Life is temporary, so build upon the rock laid so long ago.
For many before us laid their lives upon that rock.
Upon that kingdom high above us all.
The kingdom that will never fall. That kingdom intended for us all.

 Mercy

Lord Jesus, help me to understand Your mercy.
My child, My mercy is easy to understand if you try.
My mercy is like an ocean with no end—
it overflows because it cannot be contained.
It is easy to access and yet sometimes hard to find.
If the soul is willing to believe in My abundant mercy
and truly believe, then the soul can begin to search for it.
However, if the soul does not truly believe in My mercy, it will never find it.
When people are thirsty, they search for water to quench their thirst.
So, too, must they desire to search to receive My mercy.
The ones who truly believe in My abundant mercy
beg for forgiveness because they are truly sorry for their sins.
They will receive My mercy and graces to help them overcome sin.
Sometimes I allow sinners to struggle with certain sins so they depend
more on Me, and less on themselves so that they remain humble.
They must embrace these hardships as part of My mercy.
They must come to the knowledge of their sinfulness,
and move past the deceptions in their lives.
They must search for the truth, and desire the truth.
My mercy is always there waiting for them to accept it.
Sometimes they refuse to accept My mercy because of their pride.
At times they are uncertain about their desires,
torn between their worldly desires and the things of Heaven.
They must choose heavenly things over worldly things.
I know the desires of their heart and soul.
So if you want to understand My mercy, then understand Me.
I am a God of justice and mercy. I am both.
Above all things, I am a God of love.
I formed man from the dust of the earth.
When sin entered the world, the flesh became weak.
It created the need for mercy to save humanity.
It created the need for justice for the souls that went astray.
I had to give My people My laws and precepts.
Some chose to disobey and they still disobey today.
A merciful God is a just God, and a just God is a merciful God.
For mankind is frail, free to make choices, good or bad.
Free to accept or reject My love, free to obey or disobey My laws.
Free to repent and ask for My mercy.
Free to reject My ways and receive My justice.
I am a God of love, and love is merciful and just.

 The Wall

Jesus is the doorway that one must walk through to find God's peace.
We build walls right in front of the doorway.
There are those who build walls of glass.
There are those who build walls of stone.
They build walls right in front of the door that leads us to Jesus,
the only true peace they will have on this earth.
The glass wall allows us to see Jesus,
but prevents us from union with Him because of our will.
In our hearts we are sincere, but still too weak to let go.
We cannot seem to let go of the things of this world,
those very things that keep us from Him.
We try to possess these things and exist in both worlds.
The world of heavenly things; the world of earthly things.
We do not want to let go of one for the other.
When we divide our love, we minimize the benefits of our one true love.
So shatter the glass, walk through the door to your true love.
Jesus is our true love who is waiting for us.
When we build walls of stone, we cannot see the door to Jesus.
Our hearts cannot desire Jesus because we do not see Him beyond that wall.
So we live in the world, desiring things of the world, thinking we are happy.
We think that we are fine, not needing Jesus.
We think we know God, meeting Him on our terms, not His.
At least, through the wall of glass, we can see Jesus
and ask for the grace to unite with Him.
But the wall of stone forbids union with Jesus.
We stand deceived, unable to see beyond the stone wall.
We do not know the truth. We do not see the truth.
In that world there is nothing beyond the wall of stone,
no understanding of Jesus, no understanding of God's love.
Whatever wall we have built must come down,
for there is no wall that will allow us to pass through it.
It will always leave us standing on the other side forever,
unable to embrace God's love fully, unable to share in His peace.

 Christian

(A Deeper Understanding)

When I was gazing into the sky toward the heavens,
I felt the Lord looking down at me and I wondered what He felt and saw in me.
Then a thought came to me. Christian, what might you be?
So I pondered upon that word. What should a Christian be?
The word Christian begins with Christ,
which is the beginning of what a Christian is called to be:
an imitator of Christ. God is the origin of truth: Jesus is truth.
Christians have a love of God and love of neighbor.
They would not desire the things of the flesh, for that is the root of sin
which separates us from God. Sin keeps us from the truth.
Christians desire to live in Truth, which is God,
for outside of Truth are walls that keep us from God.
Christians see their own imperfections and do not accept them;
they strive for perfection in Christ through the grace of God.
Christians have a love for the Church.
Christ formed the Church. Christ is the Church.
The Church began through the apostles and by the grace of God.
The apostles led lives of poverty, charity, and selfless love.
They preached a message of repentance and conversion,
living in the truth of God, sharing His mercy and love for humanity.
True Christians live in Christ and Christ alone.
They do not seek their own benefits or needs in this world.
They live their lives desiring to do God's will, denying their own.
They live in the truth of God never misleading anyone for the love of God.
They would deny their own life for the love of another.
They desire intimacy with the one and only true love, God Himself.
They still live in the world and love all that God created.
They see the beauty in the creation of God and accept it
with gratitude, reverence, and understanding of its purpose.
Never desiring it over the creator, Himself; always thankful to the giver.
I know I will never truly understand You, Lord,
and will always wonder if I am living a life pleasing to You—
waiting for You to whisper in my ear from above.
Will You call me Christian? Will You call me friend?

 Deceiver

Let us make no mistake; let us not be easily fooled by the deceiver.
He is very real and dwells among us,
looking for ways to keep us from the love of God.
He was there in the garden of Eden.
He caused the Fall of Mankind and our first sin against God.
That first separation from God and a life of paradise here on this earth.
But the deceiver was not happy—he wanted more, so much more.
He created more ways of tempting man to keep him from God.
He continues even today with more powerful ways than ever.
He sneaks in slowly, without our knowing he is dwelling within us.
He lets us think what we are doing is innocent and harmless to our soul—
then it's too late. Consuming us until we feel completely imprisoned.
Sometimes you cannot even see it, or feel it, or even know it.
God created us to be free and, in the spirit of the Lord, you are free.
Do you ever wonder about the things we love and desire in this world?
They seem innocent enough, seem to be harmless to the soul.
In time, we find we cannot live without these idols.
If we could only understand, if we could only see.
Whichever things of this world we intensely desire
will consume our thoughts, and we will elevate them above us.
Eventually, they will control us and we will become slaves to them;
they will own us, we cannot live without them, therefore we are not free.
It is the deceiver who keeps us from the truth.
It is the deceiver who keeps us from union with God.
We are like lambs lost in the wilderness too blind to see,
not knowing the wolf is getting nearer, waiting to devour us.
The deceiver is the wolf after my soul, so it can be his for all eternity.
Keep a good watch in this world where the deceiver roams.
I was once lost. I want no longer to live with deception in my soul,
for these illusions kept me from my true love who is God alone.
To those who are too blind to see, to the souls who are misled:
You can find your way back. Look deep within yourself to who you really are.
Return back to God, and do not look back. Never look back.
For you know the deceiver's name is **Satan**.
He will not stop until you are his forever, damned in Hell for eternity.

The Mirror and Glass

Lord Jesus, help me to understand and explain this illusion.
How can one even begin to understand these images?
From the sands of the earth comes the mirror and the glass.
For the glass allows us to see clearly through it.
When we stand in front of the glass, we can see the
things in front of us and the things outside of ourselves.
Some things are pleasing to the eyes, and others are not.
We see the things of this world, but are unable to see who we are.
And, when we stand in front of the mirror, we see the exterior of ourselves
and the things that are behind us, but we cannot see inside ourselves.
For the mirror only reflects back to us what is behind us.
We see the many things that we have accumulated over time—
some we will use and some will sit collecting dust.
We cannot see who we really are, only those things that surround us.
We see so many things in the mirror and through the glass.
We can choose to look at them, or not to look at them.
Lord we see these things in front of us and behind us,
but we never really look deep within ourselves for who we really are.
We are always looking to satisfy what is outside ourselves,
seeing through the glass and mirror that which deceives our soul.
If we only would close our eyes and look deep within ourselves to who we really
are. If we would look through the glass and see things for what they really are,
then look in the mirror at the images behind us as false illusions of joy,
we would no longer stand deceived by these images.
God created us unique and beautiful, called to be Love, itself.
Has time tarnished us inside, leaving us incomplete?
We cannot change who we are looking through the glass.
We cannot change who we are looking in the mirror.
We can change who we are when we look deep within ourselves,
and open the door inside ourselves to our Savior, Jesus Christ.
Let love pour into us and let God's love pour out of us.
So how will you live the rest of your life?
Will you stare through the glass and keep dreaming of things you might want?
Will you look in the mirror and hold onto those things behind you?
Or will you look deep within, cleansing yourself, making room for God?

 Table of Unforgiveness

Many sit at the table of unforgiveness, only to deprive themselves of
the benefits of love. To eat the food of empty lies and drink the cup
of bitter hate. I have sat at this table too many times.
How my soul has felt the pain of being unforgiving to others,
causing self-inflicted wounds because of my anger.
God did not intend for us to suffer in such a way.
We are not doing God's will when we refuse to forgive one another.
Why do we give in to our selfish nature? Is it because we are too proud?
It is hard to love those that cause us pain—their words seem to pierce our soul.
In time, unforgiveness separates us from those that God loves.
Jesus gave His life for all; there is no one on this earth excluded from that.
When I think of all that Jesus suffered for the love of mankind,
it seems too hard to grasp. Jesus forgave everyone who crucified Him,
yet we find it hard to forgive those who speak poorly about us.
Just words, and we disown them, sometimes never to speak to them again.
My heart breaks when I should know better and do not forgive others.
We are all called to imitate Jesus and to grow in love for others.
We should never have enemies because we are brothers and sisters in Christ.
If brothers and sisters in Christ, then we are friends of Christ,
and if friends of Christ, we are united together in Christ.
We are all frail, born into original sin, born into imperfection,
flawed by sin, and we continue to separate ourselves from God.
We continue to choose a life of sin when we sit at the table
of unforgiveness. Not just the table of unforgiveness,
but all the tables that the devil has set for us.
At these tables there are no plates that contain the love of God—only the plates
of selfishness, greed, pride, and everything other than the love of God.
So, join me as we leave our seats at the table of unforgiveness,
and walk toward the table of unconditional love and forgiveness,
where the plates overflow, and the soul never hungers.
Where we are the welcomed guests at the table of the greatest love.
In the presence of God Almighty, and all the saints of heaven.
Where the banquet never ends and the plates will never be empty.

 Frail

What if we were able to stand in front of a mirror that would allow us to see who we really are? Would we be able to see past our exterior bodies, or is it possible we would be too blinded by the images we formed of ourselves, unable to see past our exterior body to the interior of our souls?
Does mankind stand, seduced by the world and all its empty promises?
Are we trying to satisfy our needs, attempting to please ourselves, but never able to do so? Always searching and never finding because we are empty inside.
Battling with pride, lustful hearts, and desires for worldly things.
Are we too blind to realize we are spiritually weak, trying to carry these desires that keep us from finding true joy in this world? These desires condemn us and are repulsive to our soul. One must be strong in God first, who is the ultimate and supreme ruler. If your strength is not in God, then the things of the world will tear you to pieces, leaving you empty.
For us, to rely on our own strength will not be enough.
For we are easily deceived by the things of the material world which weigh heavy on our souls, causing us to fall to our knees and to the ground we walk upon. Leaving us as frail as a stick trying to support a mountain.
The weight of the material world and its lies will crush us.
The world seduces the weak and weakens the mind to succumb to it.
Without God, we will fall hard and fast to the temptations of this world which are too strong for us to battle alone. The mind is overcome by the power of this world leaving man blinded, confused, empty and lost; unable to see the things of God and their true calling to love God and fellow man.
Who among you, if given power, wealth, and control of this world, would give it up for the love of Jesus, and live a life of poverty and humility?
I once lived a life seduced by this world and its lies.
I still struggle, but I do not struggle alone—I have Jesus Christ.
With the help of Jesus, I can now battle against the deceptions of this world, winning the battles daily, finding freedom and peace within myself.
I may never be famous, have power, or wealth.
I may never be popular, surrounded by so-called friends;
never travel the world, living my life chasing false dreams.
I will have my soul back, and to me that is all I really want.
My soul may never achieve perfection here on this earth—
none of us will. I will know and feel love again.
I will walk in the love of Jesus, and when I fall, He will lift me up.
I have something to look forward to that no one can take away from me;
I wait for the day to embrace Jesus, the true source of perfect love.

 Father

Oh Heavenly Father, I know You love all of Your creation and always will.
I know You existed before time. You existed before Creation, itself.
In Your love for us, You created the heavens and the earth;
You created everything that is and ever will be because You are Love.
Humankind will never be able to understand You, though we try.
I, myself, wonder why You created us at all because You need nothing.
It is said You need nothing from us. I myself struggle with this, Lord.
Is it wrong to say that our love for You, when it is true,
pleases You, and that You find joy when Your children show You love?
It is said that You created us because You love us,
and You created us in the image of Yourself.
Is it wrong of me to think that You created us, Your children,
because You love children? Even that thought seems hard to grasp.
We have no answers, probably never will, while here on earth; that is okay.
All I know is that You love us. Your love is the purest love,
but our love is impure, because our love for You is not true to You.
We have fallen in love with so many things of this world;
our love is divided because we choose to love so many other things.
Lord, You are constantly trying to reach us and we are too blind to see.
Throughout history, Your people have constantly let You down. However, there
have always been those faithful and devout ones who loved You so much.
I put myself among the weak ones knowing I could love You better than I do.
My prayers at times feel pointless; I wonder if they even reach the heavens.
My heart breaks because I am no different than any other person.
I know Your heart breaks too because You truly love everyone,
and would like us to love You in return—it is so little to ask of us.
We will suffer together, yet we will also suffer apart from each other.
I know my suffering helps form my soul so I can get closer to You,
but Your suffering is totally unnecessary and undeserving.
I know You are a just and merciful God who exists in perfect love;
Your justice and Your mercy are beyond our comprehension.
We are Your creation, created out of love, to love.
So in Your wisdom lies the fate of the whole human race.
Let no one be fooled—our ultimate end is in the hands of God.
Please do not abuse God's love; please do not abuse God's mercy.
Try to embrace God's love, and you will embrace Heaven for all eternity.

The Cross

Innocent was the lamb, unblemished and without sin,
pure of heart, full of the love of God, obedient until death.
Jesus, our Lord and Savior, was born as the ultimate sacrifice,
to die for the salvation of many upon a wooden cross.
Jesus became the sacrifice offered up to God out of love for mankind.
God's own people turned their faces away from God's love by rejecting His only Son, who was offered up as the sacrifice for our sins, beaten beyond recognition, spit upon and disgraced, and left to die feeling completely alone.
Jesus even felt abandoned by His Heavenly Father, and in His last moments before Jesus died on the cross, asked His Heavenly Father to forgive us.
Jesus did not die on the cross just to redeem us,
or to be the bridge to the heavenly Father—no He did not!
If that is all you want to see and are willing to accept,
you are missing out on so much more.
Jesus was showing us a life of sacrifice and love for us to imitate.
If we truly love Jesus, are we willing to die for Him?
Are we willing to sacrifice everything for Him; all our sufferings and joys?
Can we give up everything we own because we love Him?
Can we carry our crosses and unite our suffering to Jesus?
Will we be able to endure great suffering and humiliation for the love of Jesus?
Our suffering on this earth will be nothing, compared to what Jesus suffered.
Our love for others will never be enough in comparison to Jesus' love for us.
What about those days that seem to be so overwhelming?
We wonder if we can go on. You do not have to be alone. Look to the cross—
think of the weight of the sins that Jesus carried on the cross.
And, when people get mad at us, we find it hard to be silent.
Yet Jesus, "though He was harshly treated He submitted and
opened not His mouth," was silent. How hard that seems for us to do.
Jesus never did any wrong and surely did not deserve death.
He was totally innocent and full of love for the human race.
He was treated unjustly and suffered a horrible death.
None of us could ever be as innocent as Jesus was.
We will never love anyone as Jesus loves us.
None of us will ever carry a cross so heavy and so far as Jesus did.
What can we do with God's grace and God's mercy?
We can accept our crosses, which are our hardships and sufferings,
without complaining, knowing in our hearts it is because God loves us.
We must believe our crosses are for our spiritual benefit, to help us get closer to God. So embrace what is hard to love. Embrace your cross!

 Darkness

I know this place all too well, this place of darkness.
A place that once dwelt within me; it was an empty place.
I never knew of its presence until the day the Lord shined His light upon me.
I walked around in this world of darkness, living in darkness.
My soul did not even have knowledge of the darkness that dwelt within me.
Living day by day, doing the Devil's work without any knowledge of it,
living a life not pleasing to God, and thinking I was a good person.
Darkness deceives the soul, and the soul is blind to truth.
Darkness is the walking ground of the lost souls,
the home of the misled, deceived, and confused.
The blind walk around unknowing that the light is being extinguished
inside them, and the darkness gets stronger inside them.
They start to become heartless self-seekers, carrying out the works
of the evil one, and will have very little knowledge of sin or the existence of sin.
These people that dwell in darkness also form their own opinion of sin,
reject the Church's teachings, and accept false teachings.
They will live their life to what is pleasing to them and for their own gain.
When I walked in darkness, I had very little knowledge of God—
I had knowledge of God's existence, but that was not enough to sustain life.
Remember, the Devil has knowledge of God's existence, too.
The Devil exists in total darkness and wants us to be there with him.
Darkness and light cannot dwell together at the same moment in time.
Nothing good comes from a soul that is full of darkness.
No one will be completely free of the darkness because we are all sinners.
Darkness is sin, and sin dwells in everyone. Love destroys the darkness,
love is stronger than sin—in your moments of love you cannot sin.
We have a choice: to try to be the light of Christ or to continue in darkness.
I have great strength in the light of Christ; darkness no longer owns me.
I am free to love in the light of Christ and not in my selfish love—
no longer lukewarm, but on fire, being consumed by the light of Jesus.
Happiness will be achieved by those who surrender to Jesus Christ.
Those who dwell in darkness do not know the true joy of life.
Darkness only causes pain to others as well as to yourself.
Light will always prevail, even if you have to die for the truth.
You will take that light that is within you to your new home in Heaven,
where you will be consumed and completely filled with the light of Christ.
You will never know darkness; it will never have power over you again.

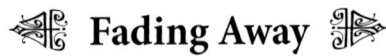 Fading Away

There was a time, long ago, when the prophets of God were true prophets. Men and women who truly understood evil for what it really was, and still is today. Prophets who took a stand against evil for the love of God and the salvation of souls. They saw the destruction evil caused the soul. They understood God as a God of love, mercy, and justice. God spoke to His prophets, who in turn spoke to God's people. They battled for truth, and died for truth, so that evil would not prevail, but there were many who refused to listen, causing them to fall away from God. God, out of love for His children, sent His only son, Jesus, to redeem the world and preach about His Father's kingdom. He was rejected, crucified, and died on a cross. The God of the Old Testament always blessed His children with much. Many took these blessings and misused them; it separated them from God. Jesus, in the New Testament, teaches everyone that we can have intimacy with God, through sacrifice, prayer, fasting, acts of mercy, and love. True prophets of God understand the meaning of the Old and the New Testaments—they do not use certain scriptures to fit their needs, attempting to meet God on their terms by twisting His words to accommodate their lifestyle. Jesus made a promise to send the Holy Spirit to give us supernatural power because man, being weak in his flesh, was unable to discern and battle evil. With the aid of the Holy Spirit, we can battle evil. Over time, evil has continued to seduce man so that many no longer desire the Holy Spirit. In time, the prophets of God slowly faded away. There are some prophets today, empowered by the Holy Spirit, still battling. The evil one appears to be gaining ground and has manipulated many to turn against God and His ways. He has deceived many, causing them to think they are equal to God, and do not need God or His church. They form their own perception of God to fit their lifestyle, resulting in the rise of false prophets, which is growing stronger every day. The true prophets are slowly fading away because the world continues to reject them. Their hearts are being crushed by the proud, disillusioned, and lost. False prophets will justify their wrongdoing, using Holy Scriptures to prove their thinking, taking certain verses from the Bible and using them to justify their lifestyle, setting a bad example to the lost and confused children of God.
This has misled many to think they do not need God's Church.
They no longer believe in sin, denying the existence and punishment for sin, choosing to believe and worship God in what is pleasing to them.
This results in the loss of intimacy with God and knowing the truth
They think God has equipped them with the power to create their own destiny. No one can control their own destiny—it is in the hands of God alone.
Seek God in Truth, through God's prophets and His great saints. All the other prophets will bring you down the road of doom and destruction.

 Purge

May you never have to undergo the trial of letting go of the flesh.
It would be better never to have chosen the road of the flesh—
how much better I would have been if I had known Jesus growing up as a child.
Why did I not listen to my parents, grandparents, and teachers of the faith?
I could have grown in knowing the love of Jesus and His ways,
but I chose the world and all its empty lies instead of the truth.
Now I have to be purged, purged of every lie I have ever lived.
I choose to follow Christ now and must be stripped of who I am.
The world and the people I love seem to be left behind.
My way of life, understanding, and everything about me belongs to Christ.
I am rejected by my loved ones at times; they do not seem to understand.
I feel like I am being ripped to pieces. I now know sin is my enemy.
I am torn between the desires of the flesh and knowing the truth.
Unable to return to my former life and letting go of everything I was,
I am being crucified in my flesh. It is a pain that cannot be described.
At times I feel alone, abandoned and rejected by those I love,
sometimes watching the world walk away from our Lord and Savior, Jesus.
I think how Your heart must be breaking, Lord, because we are too blind to see.
I remember sin used to bring me joy. Now it only brings me pain.
Now I am being purged. My flesh is being crucified, as it should be.
The world is no longer my focus. My life is no longer my own. I belong to You,
Jesus. This pain I suffer for the love of You will only be temporary.
My vision will no longer be clouded; I will be able to see again.
My Lord will continue to strengthen me so that I can carry this cross of mine.
My biggest regret is the pain that I have caused Jesus—which He did not
deserve—because of my decision to reject His sacrifice on the cross. For a lie.
My true joy awaits me in heaven when I leave this world purged of the lies,
knowing the truth, understanding that Jesus never stopped loving me and never
will. Jesus, who loves us, freely chose to give up His life to save mine.
He carried the weight of my sins upon His shoulders—upon His cross.
He laid His body on a wooden cross freely, with nails driven
through His hands and feet, because He loves me and the whole human race.
This act of love deserves nothing less than the crucifixion of my flesh!
The pains of this purging will be nothing in comparison to Your sacrifice on the
cross. I know I can never repay You.
My life is Yours, Lord; do with me what Thy will.

Worlds Apart

Forgive me, Lord. I have walked upon the face of this earth in my own world upon which I built my paradise—in a world of dreams on a foundation that crumbled under my feet. You gave me free will. I was foolish with it. I did not seek the things of God; I went in search of the things of the world. I feel like a fool, who in my own ignorance went searching for gold and ended up in a dry empty desert without spiritual food or drink.

A fool trying to draw life in a meaningless journey to nowhere in a world of empty promises, false hopes, images that lie to my soul, deceived from my true purpose of my life. You called me to be Love so that I could become Love, but I turned my face away from You and became self love.

Then You whispered in my ear and I heard Your voice calling me from out of the darkness to Your most beautiful light. Your voice tore my world apart. You left me wondering in a confused state; I had to face the lies in my world that I worked so hard to build. All the people I loved and spent most of my time with no longer knew me. Everything I ever loved crumbled before my eyes because I fell in love with You. You turned my world upside down. All that I ever loved became less appealing, without purpose—these things could no longer bring me joy. I did not know how to love You, You wanted so much more—I felt it was more than I could give You. So You went out and tested my love for You, and You whispered inside me," Who do you love more?" I replied," I love You more.

"So I left my world behind, in search of You, leaving everything I ever was in hopes of becoming a new creation in You. I chose a world of rejection for the love of You. I lived in a world between Heaven and earth, and in this new world of mine I am still unable to walk through the gates of Heaven and embrace You. I cannot see Your beautiful face nor can I share in the rewards of the heavenly promises. I cannot be with all the angels and saints. I have to survive in Your Spirit and, at times, it does not seem to be enough. The materialistic world does not understand me, so I live in a world sometimes feeling empty and alone, without human affections or love. I have nowhere to turn where I can find peace or comfort in this world. Even my prayers feel like tears falling from my eyes on the ground below me. They are unable to reach You, so I fall to my knees only to hold my tears in my hands, hoping You will take them from me and answer them. Oh Lord, there are times I do not even feel Your love. All I have are Your words to draw my strength, to survive. Sometimes even Your words cannot pierce the emptiness I feel inside myself. So I close my eyes in hopes of awakening to the joy I feel when You are with me, thinking back on those moments that we shared in Your precious love, trying so hard not to forget that love we shared. You, Oh Lord, know how hard I have tried! We may be worlds apart now, however I know this is only temporary. Let me draw strength in Your Spirit and Your love for I will leave this world with no regrets; I will leave nothing behind that can keep me from You. My world and Your world will be one.

Darkness and Light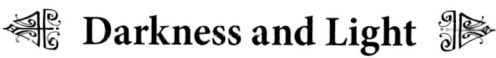

We are born into darkness and baptized into the light of God.
When we entered this world we inherited the sins of Adam and Eve.
We inherited the desire to sin, known as our fallen nature.
This nature we will battle the rest of our lives, against the world of
darkness, unaware of the damage it could be causing to our souls.
As children the small things we do seem to be harmless to the soul—
getting things our way, the small fights, and people spoiling us,
the things of the flesh—all appear innocent enough.
These are the things that began to form us into the world of darkness
and the world of darkness does not know true love which is God's light.
As we grew older, we freely chose to enter darkness or the light,
and if we are formed in the darkness at an early age, we will barely see the light.
The world today teaches us to love and please ourselves over all things.
We have grown without an understanding of what the true light is;
some of us even think that God's light is really within us.
So what is this light I talk about? God is the light which emits true and pure love.
This can be found in a pure heart filled with the love of God.
God loves the humble of heart and the humble can see the light.
The proud of heart dwell in the world of darkness, far away from the light.
The merciful, the charitable, the forgiving, are gentle of heart,
full of compassion, full of love, and full of the light of God.
The heartless, the selfish, the unforgiving, the merciless,
the takers, the greedy, the arrogant—all dwell in darkness.
Light and darkness can exist in the soul together, but only one will surface
at a time, which will be revealed by how we treat others at that point in time.
We must try, with God's mercy and grace, to exist in the total light
and to eliminate the darkness that dwells within our soul.
I know the world of darkness too well—it dwelt within me far too long.
Through the prayers of many and the mercy of God, the light entered into my
soul. I continue to search for the light of God which is truth and love.
We can continue to think we dwell in the light—believe me I thought I did.
We are not perfect because we are human—there will always be darkness
within us—and in those moments of darkness we will deny the light of God's love.
As we grow in the light, we see more of the darkness within ourselves,
our vision becomes clearer, and we see things through the light of God's eyes.
Let us move into humility, for there you can find the light and the truth.
You can move away from the darkness of your soul into the beautiful light;
you can share in the joy of the Lord here on this earth;
you can be the light of Jesus and shine in the world of darkness;
you can bring hope to a world in so much need of God's love.
So go out and shine—let the light of Jesus inside you radiate to the world!

Letting Go

Who among you can let go and truly desire Heaven?
Most feel the need to accomplish much here
and yet focus so little on getting ready for the next life.
You need to grow stronger in your relationship with Me.
I will prepare you for Heaven if you are willing to let go.
Do not be afraid; it is okay. I am really here, you just need to
believe—just let go of yourself from this world and all your desires.
Picture in your mind that you stand between Heaven and Hell;
that your life is hanging in the balance, based on your decisions—
the desires of your heart and your love for Me and My people.
Do you know that Hell is below you and Heaven is above you?
Envision that every decision you make is moving you closer,
closer to the place where you will spend the rest of your life.
Know that sin separates you from Me, it moves you away from Me.
Know that I am in Heaven trying to draw you closer to Me. Your sins offend Me;
they cause Me much suffering. In time your sins keep you from knowing Me.
Do you believe in your heart you are falling away from Heaven because of sin?
Have you ever thought of spending eternity in Hell?
Close your eyes, open your mind, and take a look below you.
All you will see is the suffering of many souls. Such great torment,
pain beyond human thought, and an eternity longing to be with Me.
Never to feel or embrace the depth of My pure love;
only the desires of the flesh and your sins that put you there.
Close your eyes, open your mind, and look above you.
You should begin to feel My love and want to begin to embrace it.
There is nothing in this world like it because it is not of this world.
My love is unending, and when the soul immerses itself into My love,
it will achieve ecstasy beyond human thought and emotion.
The joys of this world can never compare with the things of Heaven.
The desires you experience here will seem meaningless and empty
in comparison to Heaven. Is living a sinful life worth an eternity in Hell?
It will take time, sometimes a lifetime, to let go of your desires for this world.
You must keep trying. I know your heart and understand your weaknesses.
Fight the good fight, trust in Me, and you will make it to Heaven's door.
Always remember never to turn back, no matter how hard it may seem.
I will give you the grace. I will never abandon you. I will always be there.

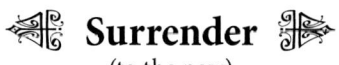 Surrender
(to the now)

You, Lord, are the lover of all souls and deserve more than what I give You.
For years I thought I could do everything without Your help—
I was wrong. I did not want to find You and I did not want Your help.
I was a proud man. A man of this world. A foolish man.
At the time, the world offered me so much, so I thought.
It seemed You had very little to offer. How blind I was.
I had all the answers and listened to no one; too proud to accept help.
Somehow Your light entered my miserable soul just enough
to go looking for You.
I continued my search for You, knowing Your love is always true;
Your love will never forsake me or abandon me.
You have blessed me with so much and will always continue to bless me.
Lord, for what little love I give You, You deserve so much more.
The decisions I have made in the past have separated me from You.
I submitted myself to the sins of this world which I freely embraced,
surrendering my will to the road that led my soul to
destruction—to a place far away from You, Oh Lord.
In Your stream of unending love, You poured love out upon my miserable soul.
You washed me clean, and let me bathe in Your pool of unending love.
I am not perfect. I will always be a sinner, constantly in need of Your protection,
always knowing Your love will carry me through the highs and lows in my life.
So upon this paper, I confess my frailties and admit my weaknesses,
knowing I can do nothing without You, surrendering my will to Your will.
In this moment, I surrender my broken will to You, Lord.
How beautiful this surrender feels—my imperfect will uniting with Your perfect will.
Not as a slave to Your love, or imprisoned by Your love. No, Lord!
In my surrender, let it be a testimony of the freedom and joy I now have.
No longer a prisoner of this world, but a free man, a slave to Christ.
A prisoner of pure love, compassion, mercy, and forgiveness.
A testimony to my Lord, who saved me from the fires of Hell and a life of eternal
damnation. I deserved nothing and You gave me all.
I have the hope of someday spending eternity in Heaven with You.
Here I am frail and broken, deserving of nothing. **I surrender.**

Amen

 Death

The day will come when I will no longer awake—
never to open my eyes and see this world again.
The day will come for you, as well—for everyone.
I see death differently now, not like I did years ago.
Before I came to know Jesus and to grow in faith and love,
I was already dead and I did not even know it.
I was dead to Christ and the knowledge of His love for us—
too blinded by this world and what it appeared to offer.
By the mercy and love of Jesus, I live in a new life.
The words of Jesus have taught me to die to myself,
and live a new life in Jesus, and in Him alone.
My greatest fear is to deny my Lord and Savior, Jesus.
I asked for the grace never to deny my Lord under persecution,
and when Death is knocking at my door I will open it,
knowing that Jesus will be waiting for me on the other side.
I thought back when death would take me away from everything,
but now I know death will free me from everything here.
I do not look at Death as my enemy but as a welcomed friend.
There are certain individuals who look at death as the ultimate end,
who reject the things of God and His love for them; they think
there is no afterlife, no Heaven and no Hell. They believe it will be an
earthly end where their bodies are buried in the ground left to rot away.
It is sad, but true: their bodies will remain in the ground never to see the
resurrection of life, never to have their souls unite with their glorified
bodies. Their souls will leave their bodies behind forever.
God will pass His judgment on these poor souls who may end up in Hell,
and if they do, will live eternity in a life of torment, in true death.
Let the only death we fear be spending a lifetime in Hell.
May I spend the rest of my life doing the will of God,
so that when Death comes knocking at my door I will open it
as a welcomed friend. I will embrace my true love, Jesus.
I will no longer chase imperfect love, empty dreams, and false hopes.
Remember, if you are part of this world, Death will never be your friend;
but if you focus on Heaven, Death will be a welcomed friend.
You will be able to say, **"Oh Death, my friend, take me home to Jesus."**

 Holding On

Your ways of living life, O Lord, are far better than my understanding of life. I am constantly searching, trying to understand how to live the life You want me to live. My memories of the pleasures I once searched for now imprison my soul, making it harder to let go of the desires of my past. They appear to be part of me, and I want them to go away. My sins, which I welcomed without knowledge, entered the house of my soul. I was blinded by these sins that pierced my soul; they stayed with me, continually blinding and tormenting me. I foolishly allowed sin to set up rooms in the house of my soul. Lord, I did not know You when I allowed them into the house of my soul.
These unwelcomed guests do not want to leave—they want to take control of my soul, and keep me from loving You and Your ways. I thought I was holding onto them, only realizing they were holding onto me. We are entangled in a web of right and wrong and need to be separated—one pulling on the other, constantly tugging at my emotions and thoughts. The good versus the evil. My body and soul wish I had never invited them into my life. These evil spirits and their sinful ways torment my mind and soul at will without warning. I find myself sometimes holding onto these spirits because my memory reminds me of the pleasure they brought to my flesh. At times, I cannot separate the things I have been holding onto from the things I need to let go.
I feel so foolish, Lord, because You have given me the wisdom and understanding to discern the harm that sin causes my soul. Yet my sin appears to be so appealing to my flesh that I desire it over pleasing You. O Lord, in that moment when sin overtakes me, I think nothing of the hurt it causes You. Satan's deception keeps me from seeing the truth. Only after the sinful act, do I feel the pain of disappointment because I let You down. I feel the guilt and sorrow because I offended You.
You, O Lord, who are always searching my heart, as You search everyone's heart, know me inside and out. You know if I desire Your ways or not. You know if I truly desire to follow Your ways and precepts and live in Your truth. I am weak, holding onto my sinful ways which battle against my desire to please You. I lack the graces necessary to overcome my desires and weaknesses that cause me to sin. You know in my heart and soul, if I could, I would never fail You. How often I wanted to love You, Lord—I wish I had known You earlier in my life. I wish the world never took me from Your loving arms. I will battle the lies of my past, the demons and sins of long ago. With Your grace, I will fight against the things I hold onto. I am a flower in need of watering—shower Your love upon me. Let me grow in Your garden of love. Wash the dirt from my petals and make me clean again. O Lord, let the only things I ever desire be pleasing to You.

 Time

None of us can escape time in this world for our life is in the hands of time. God created time and the world we live in, a world moving in time. Each one of us has received a cup—some a short cup, some a tall one. We all drink of the cup of time and, when the last drop of time is gone, our life goes with it. Some say it is not fair that they receive such a short cup. Some feel their cup is too tall because of hardships and sufferings in their life. Who am I to question the cup that God has given me to drink? Some say time has no friends and waits for no one. This may be true, or is it? Charity does not know time because charity does not watch time. Charity is love. Because it loves, it moves through time unaware of itself moving. Greed knows time all too well. It does not want to waste any time because its fortune dwindles in every second that is lost. The ones who know Jesus are not troubled by time or lack of time. Their trust is in God and not in themselves; they do not rejoice in time, nor do they fear time. They exist in time trusting in the Creator of Time. But woe to the people of the world who live in fear of time running out. They will spend the rest of their life trying to beat time. They never will! They will fear everything that takes time from them: unexpected death, diseases, and all the things that can take life away from them. Some people, when life on this earth is over, believe their bodies will remain in the ground here on this earth, no longer existing because they think there is no afterlife. Living their lives, bathing in the world of temporary joys, drinking their time away, they are focused on things that will take them away from their heavenly promise to the empty world below. The true servant and good keeper of time will use it wisely to do the things that the master has called them to do. They will wake every morning thankful for another day and, when evening comes, they will give praise for the blessings and the hardships that God allowed. For when those who love God see their cup of life is running out, they will not grumble or complain. They will praise God for every drop they receive, understanding in their hearts and souls that the cup they receive was poured out from a cup of love. This love hung upon a cross, and His blood was shed for many so that death and time would no longer imprison them. They know Jesus died for the forgiveness of our sins, giving us new hope in the resurrection of life. Oh Time, my friend, I will not miss you if I make it through Heaven's doors. I will no longer know you and you will no longer exist, for your creator will no longer need you in this new world. I pray that I have used you well in my life and, when the last drop touches my lips, we will say goodbye forever. I thank you, my friend, for helping me reach Heaven's doors. Whether the cup was short or tall, it did not really matter.

Search My Heart

O Lord, search my heart; You will not always find the true me by my actions. Sometimes, my mouth speaks unkind words to Your children, and I know that You love them so much. At times, I lack compassion for those You love. I am not always a good example of what a Christian should be; I am weak and have failed You so many times. More often than I should. Often I feel like Judas, Your betrayer, when I am rejecting Your love. How many times have You been there with me, and I turned my back on You? How many times have I failed to profess Your name because I was afraid or ashamed of You? Perhaps I was too concerned of what people would think of me if I spoke about Your love for them, or how You died because You loved them, or how their sins separate them from You, causing You so much pain. My sins offend You! Deep in my heart I know this is true. Does it concern me enough to stop sinning and offending You? I just carry on like a careless lover whose only concern is my own selfish needs and wants.

My soul suffers from the loss of Your love because I feel unworthy of it. I travel through the dark night of my soul, feeling like a child abandoned by his mother, crying out to the heavens and hearing no response.

My prayers bring no comfort, no consolation can be found. Part of me is madly in love with You, while the other part of me is betraying You. Without Your grace, I am nothing. Until I come to my nothingness, You will receive even less of what I am—a miserable sinner drowning in his own sorrow.

When I come to my nothingness, I will totally rely on You, not myself. You will become my strength, my fortress, the rock upon which I stand. I will no longer stand alone in my weaknesses, but draw my strength from You. Do not search my heart in my frailties and faults; You will not find me there. Search my heart when I am feeling Your presence so strong inside me; in that moment when You are my only love, and nothing else matters. Search my heart when You are my everything and nothing can take Your place. Not when I am letting You down because I am imperfect and lacking grace.

I know You already know that, but sometimes I just forget. We think we know it all and have it all figured out—we are so wrong! We let our pride get in the way of knowing the truth of who we really are. I was afraid of facing the truth about my weaknesses—worried about what the world would think of me—then I realized it did not matter. The only thing that matters is what You think of me. What the world thinks of me will not save me.

Let what is in the depth of my heart be the only thing that You ever see. Never look outside my heart, for part of me will always let You down. Deep in my heart, I really do love You. I am sorry for all the pain I have caused You and the pain I will cause You. My heart is Yours and will always be Yours, even when everything else outside my heart is betraying You.

 My Eyes

My Lord, You taught us to open our eyes so that we can see.
When I came into existence, I opened my eyes to this world,
too young to understand my real purpose in life, too innocent
to see and know evil. Unable to separate the darkness from light,
I was a child in the hands of the world waiting to be formed
like a leaf tossed around in the wind at the mercy and grip of the human race.
Potters molding me like clay in their image of what a person ought to be,
they were part of my life. I put my trust in them, not knowing God.
They had the power to show me the world of darkness and light,
teaching me to live in the ways of sin or the ways of the Church and truth.
I was raised in the love of God but never saw the world of light.
Even though my eyes were opened, I was blinded from seeing the truth.
The darkness in my life and my sinfulness kept me from seeing the light.
I walked and stumbled through life because I could not see the light.
Darkness surrounded me because I chose to let it in—it was so appealing to my
flesh—and what little light my soul could see was not enough to save me.
So my soul clung to what little light it had—a small dot of light in a body
consumed with darkness—unaware of the light of Jesus Christ, my Lord and
Savior. I plunged into the world of darkness. I felt so alone and incomplete.
My soul, in desperation, taking its last breath, cried out to the heavens.
The Light heard my words and poured out its mercy upon my miserable soul.
The heavens opened up and showered His light all over me.
It washed the darkness from my flesh,
that which kept the Light from entering my soul.
The lungs of my soul were filled with the breath of life from the new Light.
The Light broke through the wall of darkness, and the Light flowed into my body
and into my eyes. I saw God's creation with new eyes and hope for a new life.
The beauty of the Light filled my heart and soul with joy and true peace.
I began to grow in strength and wisdom of the things of God and began to look
past the walls of darkness, seeing the truth that was hidden behind them.
I saw sin for what it really was and called to Heaven for graces to overcome sin.
I saw my selfish nature and the ugliness of my flesh and its desires.
With my new eyes, I saw the Truth and the Light. My flesh and soul became one
in union with the Light, no longer fighting against each other,
but working together as one in union with our Lord.
The Light is beautiful beyond description and our minds cannot understand.
I find the darkness is no longer appealing, but the darkness still torments me,
trying to win me back, always seducing my mind, in hopes of bringing me to the
underworld forever. My strength is in my love for the Light that allows me to
battle against the darkness. There can be no darkness where there is Light.
My eyes have seen the true beauty of the Light.
May I never turn back and see the world of darkness again.
Let those who have eyes see!

 Pure of Heart

The Servant:

O Lord, hear my cry; let my words reach Your ears. Guide me; show me Your ways because Your love is true. I am afraid we might have forgotten how to love You, forgotten how to sacrifice, forgotten how to love others as ourselves. Are we corrupting our children because we give them everything of this world? Do we fail to teach them who You are and Your commandments? Can we ever love like children again? Is our childlike innocence lost forever? Tell me, Lord, what I must do to be pure of heart? I want to love You wholeheartedly. Do not hold Your words back from me; I need to hear them. Your words are merciful, just, and true. Spare me no judgment; I have failed You.

Our Lord:

A heart cannot be pure when it desires sinful things. You must fight against the very things that corrupt your heart—they only leave you bleeding in a pool of suffering, drowning in the misery of your own wretched soul.
You will be discontent, constantly searching for Me, wondering why I am not listening. It is you who is not listening. You know the road to Me and still sway from Me because of your foolish passions and desires.
Arise, O sleeper, from your bed of deception, and try harder to see the truth. What love on this earth can satisfy you and fill the voids of your heart? You wish to be pure of heart—only pure love can do this. Let go of your selfish desires and needs. Let go of your false hopes and dreams.
Search for Me, and Me alone—nothing else will satisfy you.
Do not pretend to be blind—you have eyes to see—open them.
Let My light pierce your soul to the very core. Let it consume you in its entirety. Do not allow yourself to be half-hearted in receiving My light; be fully open to it. I love you enough to allow you to suffer. Through your suffering you will see the need for Me and rely on Me alone. Your empty love will be made full.
Your pride allows you to act in an unkindly way towards others and harms your own soul. Your selfishness takes from others giving yourself more of what you do not need, leaving you more empty than before you began.
Your anger does not only hurt others, but it hurts Me who dwells inside them. Your foolish desires never benefit anyone, not even yourself.
To be the purest of heart you must dwell in the places where My love is, not wandering in places far from it. You can not drift back and forth in the world— try to remain in My light. Do not let the darkness pull you in. Let My love build walls around you to keep the enemy from harming and deceiving you.
The Devil cannot live in a heart that loves. Always be open to receiving My grace. Desire nothing of this world. Accept and carry your cross.
Seek the kingdom of heaven. Come to your nothingness and you will be filled with the things of Me. The purest of heart can only be found in the truest of love— nothing else will do.

 Walk With Me

My son, walk with Me just a little further. You do not have far to go! I know you are growing tired and your journey seems long—sometimes even pointless. Open your heart just a little wider and trust in Me. I was there when you turned your back on Me and left Me. I never left you; I was right by your side though you could not feel Me. I felt the emptiness in your heart and your soul. I watched you walk through the forest, lost and confused. I watched you walk through the desert, thirsting for water, unable to drink. I watched you scratch the desert sand, but you could not find the living water. You climbed the highest mountain and thought I was not there. You sailed across the oceans, never finding what you were looking for. You never found a place to rest, until you finally chose to rest in Me. You never had a place to call home; now you know where to look. I loved you enough to let you wander in the wilderness of this life. I opened all the doors for you and watched you walk by them. You grew tired of walking; you called out My name; I picked you up. You asked Me, "Why did you wait so long to pick me up?" I answered you, "Why did you wait so long to ask Me for help?" I picked you up and dusted the dirt off you; I made you clean again. You no longer walk in the world of darkness feeling all alone; now you walk in My light. You will never feel alone—you will know **I Am**. I did not say the road would be easy; it comes with much suffering. There will be those who will persecute you and some will hate you and condemn you. The world that rejected Me will reject you because of the love you have for Me. My grace will give you life. My light will guide you on the road you walk. Your enemies will cause you no harm. I will fill your mind with the wisdom of Heaven. You will live in My peace and no one can take that from you. Pick up your cross and follow in My footsteps on your road to Heaven. Do not ever look back. There is no place you can return to. There is nowhere you can call home. There is nowhere to rest your head. You have only Me. Walk with Me, hand in hand, and together we will do great things. We will climb the highest mountains. We will cross the oceans to the ends of the earth. We will gaze at the stars together beyond the universe towards the heavens. You will leave all your suffering behind that you carried for so long. Your walk on this earth will seem like a blink of an eye. You can leave your cross at the door; you will not be needing it anymore. The door will be open—come on in. Walk with Me as we walk side by side for all eternity.

 Obstacles

In our unending search for the truth, we must pass through a series of obstacles. The truth is in front of us...behind us...the truth is all around us. The depth of our soul should desire to know the truth, which is God.
In our journey, which will eventually end in death, we must seriously consider whether we are truly searching for the truth in its entirety, or only partial truth.
In this age of modern-day thinkers, many say truth is relative.
If truth is relative, it would deny what truth really is, for truth must have an origin. It cannot be changed or modified, otherwise it no longer remains truth.
It becomes a supposed truth. God is truth—He existed before time and space.
Anything outside of the truth becomes an obstacle to freedom; not knowing or denying the truth becomes a great obstacle in our lives.
It is said that we cannot find the truth, but the truth will find us.
In our journey, as we search to make sense of our lives, we try to understand our own existence and our purpose in life. We come up with more questions than answers. More walls than openings. Why does life seem so complicated?
The truth is, we make our lives more complicated than they have to be.
We are the ones who put the obstacles in our way.
God created us to be free, not bound or imprisoned by anything, He does not put obstacles in front of us to slow us down, nor does He burden us with excessive weight. He is a God of love, not a God of slavery or imprisonment.
So how do I find freedom in a world full of materialism, self-love, instant gratification, need for power and wealth, and sins of all kinds?
Freedom is found in God's love and nowhere else. His love does not imprison you. It does not control you. It does not own you. It does not possess you.
If nothing can imprison God, then how can you be imprisoned by God's love?
If God is free, you are free when you dwell in his love because you are part of Him. You are free to reject or accept His love, which means you are free to live in His love or to live outside of it: He never forces His love on anyone.
The obstacles in our lives are put there by us when we live outside of God's love—when we choose to take control of our own lives and put God second.
Only when you come to your nothingness and realize, by your own strength, you are nothing—only then, in Jesus, can you do all things. Everything you are is through Him, and Him alone. I know we all want to feel like we are in control of our lives and our destiny, and to some degree that might be true. But eventually we have to believe God is in control of our lives or we will choose to believe in a so-called truth, and believe in our hearts they are true, when they are really false.
We have free will to make our own choices, but also free will to put obstacles in front of ourselves that will lead us down paths of hardship and unnecessary suffering. I am asking you to search your heart and soul; that is where you will find the doorway to the truth in its entirety. That is where God placed part of Himself—in your heart. He is waiting for you to open your heart to Him.
Will you open up your heart to God and let the truth come into you?

The Journey

My journey began inside the womb of my mother where God's thoughts created me, and placed me with His hand in the channel of my mother's body. I lived and grew in a world surrounded by liquid and a thin wall inside my mother's womb, with a tube that sustained and nourished my body. I was not alone, Lord, You were with me and Your spirit was within me. My life depended on my mother's health and her safety; she was my lifeline. The day came for me to leave that world and enter a world unknown to me. I exited my mother's body into the hands of strangers. They cut the cord which sustained my life and slapped me, hoping to give me new life apart from my mother. I was too frail and needed the help of many to guide me and nourish me in this new environment. You were there, Lord, looking down upon me from the heavens. You never let me out of Your sight. Eventually, I became a man and the time came for me to move on. I sailed across an ocean of dreams, landed on the shores of illusion, in a land of promises containing valleys and mountains which my emotions would respond to. In that place, I relied on my senses, allowing me to fall into sin. You were never part of my thoughts. I continually gave into my senses and my soul was conquered without knowledge—my soul was dying. I eventually climbed the mountain of sin. The higher I climbed, the darker it became and I was surrounded by darkness. One day, while on this mountain, a light pierced through the darkness coming from the heavens. I saw my emptiness and decided to descend the mountain and walk across the desert of despair. From a distance I saw a well and headed for it; I heard a voice say, "Drink of the living water." I drank from it. The water gave me life. I turned back to see the world I left behind, which seemed obscure and far away. I knew I could not return to that place. I looked forward and saw many crosses on the ground along the side of the path. The path went up the mountain as far as I could see, towards the heavens. Then the voice spoke to me and told me to walk along the path and pick up a cross and carry it until I reached the next cross. I was to put the cross down along the path and pick up another cross, and I was to keep doing this until I reached the top of the mountain. The voice said that these crosses would make me stronger, wiser, and more appreciative of the things I have been blessed with. The voice also said the crosses I carried would allow me to draw closer to His son, Jesus. His son carried the cross that bore the sins of the world. In this union, I would experience a great peace within me and live in the joy of the Lord. I would never desire to go back; there was nothing to return to. Every day is a new day with one purpose: to serve the Lord the best I can, without grumbling and complaining about the cross I have to carry. I understand it will make me stronger. Without it, I would fall back to the world I left so long ago. I walk with God by my side; sometimes He carries me when I am feeling weak, unable to go on by my own strength. I try to follow His footsteps, avoiding as much as possible getting in front of Him. I try to trust in His guidance, knowing He knows what is best for me. At the end of this journey, I hope to spend a lifetime with all the angels and saints in a world existing in perfect harmony with our God.

 Castles

Most of us fail to see the enemy breaking through the walls of our exterior castle—our bodies—of which we are the keepers, meant to be kept pure and holy before God. Our souls are the interior castle which the Devil will try to enter and destroy. He must get past the exterior castle first, through manipulation, causing us to sin. The Devil is shrewd and finds many ways to break through the exterior walls. He will try to deceive us through our senses because that is what we respond to the most. Sometimes our emotions interfere with the decisions we should make. We attempt to satisfy our senses without considering the damage it might cause by weakening our exterior walls, allowing the enemy to enter the interior of our souls. These walls will crumble without our knowing, and the Deceiver will enter the interior of our souls, destroying the castle from within. We must be vigilant in guarding the exterior walls, for it is through the desires of the flesh and sin that the Devil enters the interior of our souls.

We rely too much on satisfying and fulfilling the needs of our senses.

Our love for God is the fortress and the walls of the interior castle.

Our pride, selfishness, and instant gratification are the enemies to the interior castle. They will plant their roots at the outside walls, where they grow and expand, slowly and constantly penetrating the walls of the exterior castle.

We think that by satisfying our senses we have achieved happiness, and continue on that road without giving a thought to how it is damaging to us.

Eventually, we lose the connection to God that is needed, causing us to fall deeper into sin and further away from God, upsetting the balance necessary to achieve a union with God. If this union is not achieved by the time the body and soul depart from each other in death, the soul might not reunite with the body in a glorified state in the resurrection of life, because the soul may be damned for all eternity. The interior life is your only hope of achieving true peace and union with God here on Earth. A strong interior castle can supply life to the exterior castle. The interior and exterior are one—body and soul. The stronger the interior life is, the stronger the flesh is able to resist sin. If the human heart, small in size, is properly maintained, it gives the body great strength and endurance throughout a lifetime. So it is with the interior life that glorifies God through our bodies. Conversely, a heart that is not taken care of properly causes the body to become weakened, barely sustaining life, leaving the individual with physical suffering and emotional misery. The interior life, unattended, will lead our body into sin and separation from God, into a world of darkness. The Devil cannot pass through the walls unless you allow him; he cannot destroy your body until he has destroyed your heart and soul. The Devil will try to seduce the mind, knowing that by entering your mind he can destroy the exterior through sin and self-love. By penetrating the walls of the interior and destroying the love that dwells in the interior castle, he leaves the individual in a world of rubble and ashes, swept up by the winds of eternal damnation. The choice is yours.

Measurement of Love

If love could be measured by a cup, how would it be measured?
It would be measured by the size of the cup, the volume inside, the purity of the substance, and the outpouring of the cup.
Each one of us has the capacity to love, depending on how much our love is mixed with selfish love. The mixture of these different kinds of love exists in all of us; there are no exceptions. We are all flawed because of our selfish love.
We all have different sized cups from which our love is poured.
Some cups are great in size: these contain works of charity, acts of mercy, and unconditional and sacrificial love. Some cups appear to be small: these contain just a few drops of unselfish love. The rest of the cup is filled with selfish love, pride, and bitter hate. On this earth, we will never be able to hold a cup that will contain pure love because our love is corrupted by our broken nature.
Do not be discouraged; we have hope, a source from which we can draw.
A source of pure, uncorrupted love with no end.
It flows from an ocean of love that is not contained or limited by anything.
The human mind cannot conceive nor understand this unlimited source of love.
We know in our hearts of its existence and that we need to desire to drink from this cup of unending love. It is the only love that can help us to purify our love.
God's cup consists of many ingredients and its mixtures baffle the human mind.
It contains His unending love, His mercy, His justice, His anger, and His suffering. This mixture, which contains only love, is not contaminated by a single drop of selfish love. It is one-of-a-kind—there is nothing like it in the whole universe. It can never be equaled or matched by anything or anyone.
It is hard for us to understand that in God's anger and justice we should feel loved and know His actions are filled with unending love for you and me.
God's love is not measured by the same standards that we measure our love.
Our understanding of love is not true to the real meaning of love.
Our love contains emotions and feelings which are tainted by selfish love.
God's love is not tainted or corrupted by human feelings and emotions.
It is so important that we draw life and drink from the cup of His unending love.
If we continue trying to draw life from a cup that contains the poisons of this world, we will die a slow death, breath by breath, until our bodies and souls reach spiritual death. We will dry up and wither away, dead from spiritual dehydration.
The cup of darkness never allows you to see beyond the rim of the cup you drink; its darkness and obscurity keeps you from seeing the truth and the depth of God's love. The cup of life allows you to see beyond the rim and into its depths, to which there is no end. His love is light, which allows you to see with clearer eyes; the more you drink of this cup the more you see and understand the truth. If you search the depth of your soul, it will thirst for this cup.
Drink up, it is free—you will not thirst anymore because this cup has no end.

 Our Hearts

At one time in my life, I fell in love. Or at least with what I perceived to be love. Along with that type of love, came the responsibility of satisfying someone else's needs as well as satisfying my own. This love entailed responsibility and sacrifice which at times was difficult. We became one through marriage and yet remained very much individuals. I did not have a strong foundation in Jesus Christ, and what I thought was love was not truly love, but a love distorted by lust and self-love. I did not understand what true love was and it's true meaning.

I perceived love to be what the world taught me it was supposed to be. My heart was unable to know what true love was until it became filled with God's love. My perception of love was to grow together, acquiring material things. My spouse and I had no concerns about the love of Christ, nor did we care. We only existed in the world's perception of love consisting of conquering others in the world, competing in a race against time, against each other for worldly possessions, notoriety, money, and power. We had no remorse or respect for one another. Everything became a trophy to place on our mantle.

Over time, my heart became cold and insensitive; its only purpose was to satisfy my own needs. I did not care about anyone else's needs or successes.

I became a conqueror and gloated about people's misery and suffering. Darkness filled my soul and my body plunged into sin. I felt no sorrow, no guilt, no remorse. I felt nothing—I was dead inside as my physical body maintained life. What can a heart tell you when it has no understanding of what true love is? It tells you everything and anything but the truth. It creates an image of what love is supposed to be. It misleads you down the road far away from true love.

I know the emptiness and the heartbreak that comes with the love that is not true. I spent my life searching for love in materialism and the sinful things of this world, only to come up short. I was lost and blinded, totally naïve and ignorant to love. Our Lord and Savior saw me in such a pitiful state, His heart must have torn into two. But He never stopped loving me. Many were praying for me, and God heard their prayers. God answered them. God's love entered my heart and my eyes were opened. I was no longer blind and began to see through the eyes of love. I no longer spend time searching to satisfy my needs through things that brought me temporary joys, that only lasted for brief moments. No longer struggling, trying to satisfy my senses. I never felt satisfied. I was always thirsting, always searching, and never finding, always wanting. You do not have to spend a lifetime going down an empty road in search of love. All you have to do is open your hearts and ask for it. God's love is true, it is pure, it is unconditional without end.

Save Me

Words cannot describe the sorrow I feel in my soul because of the remnants of the sins that remain within me; the tormentors of my joy and peace in the Lord. Shadows and walls of darkness fill my soul with emptiness, leaving me feeling incomplete. False humility overshadowed by pride creates illusions that deceive my soul, leaving me unable to see who I really am, and who I am to be.
Empty thoughts that never amount to anything, always falling short of my true calling, leave me unable to accomplish those things for the glory of God.
Desire for things that give me temporary satisfaction, searching to fulfill my needs through avenues that are as temporary as the rest of my desires, leave me feeling upside down and paralyzed, trying to get back on my feet so that I can stand upright.
My perception is obscured for lack of light because of the darkness that surrounds my soul. Every sin, regardless of how small, blocks the light from entering the shell of my body and reaching my soul. The darkness affects the clarity of the vision ahead of me, leaving me walking around blind and stumbling across a path that contains the truth of who I am—who I am supposed to be.
Oh, my Lord and Savior, hear my prayers and petitions as I stand before You. In such a wretched state, I walked around blind, unable to see who I am. I know I still have a long road ahead of me; I can only see the road as You continue to pour out Your graces upon me. Your grace is also the light that shines upon my soul, allowing me to look inward to the depths of my soul.
Your grace remains a mystery and without it we can accomplish nothing. There were many times I failed to ask You for Your grace; I thought I could do it on my own. Without it I would have remained in darkness forever.
For years I closed the door on Your grace. I imprisoned my soul in a world far away from You in my house of sin surrounded by the darkness with the devil as my friend who shared his wonderful stories of how life was supposed to be. His words were filled with empty promises and lies, but he had a way about him that persuaded me to do many things. He was clever and created a world that seemed so appealing to my eyes which I could not resist, and he hid the truth from me. Then one day, You knocked at my door and Your light entered my room. I saw the devil for who he really was. I saw his lies and all the images he created within me. Lord, You saved me that day—I can never repay You. I need you Lord; I will always need You. The devil will not let go of me; he wants me all for himself. I spent many years in his company living a lifestyle of sin. The memories and the lies keep tormenting me, calling me back away from You, constantly calling me back to the world I am trying to leave behind. Lord, it is so hard when I know the truth. Forgive me; my heart keeps forgetting that You should be the most important part of my life. Will You keep showering Your graces upon me and save me, please save me?

 Arena

Over time, God's sorrow found its way into the depth of my soul leaving me in despair. The eyes of my soul saw with clarity the depth of sin in my own soul as well as the sinfulness in the world I live in. Words cannot describe the emptiness I felt—it broke my heart. With His grace, I have chosen the road that allows me to love God as much as is humanly possible. There are many in this world who have chosen to love the world over God; they have chosen to love the lesser of the two. I now walk in an arena, although not in the physical sense. In this arena, I am persecuted because I have chosen to love God above all things. At one time, there were real arenas into which many devout Christians were dragged because of their love of God, sacrificing their own lives. I have been spared of that, but am persecuted by people's thoughts and words and sometimes hated because of my love of Christ. They refuse to hear my words or understand me.

There are two other arenas in this world bigger than the arena I live in. The sports arenas of this world are the next largest with millions of spectators. Many attend these arenas and watch their gladiators play against each other for victory over each other. Some watch these events through man-made vessels which allow them to see their gladiators from the convenience of their own home. I call these playing fields, "arenas of glory." Many will sit back in drunken sinfulness, cheering their teams on while they scream and curse at the other gladiators. They let their emotions carry them away without a care in the world, and without realizing they drag themselves down to the world of self-indulgence as their senses begin to escalate and their souls begin to decline.

The third arena is the greatest and biggest of them all. In this arena, God is the spectator looking down upon the earth at His children who inhabit it.

Let us not forget that the eyes of heaven are gazing upon us. There is no one who can hide from heaven's view. How we act and what we do is seen from above. Millions of sins are seen from above while we try to conquer one another in the competition of life. Without remorse, we think nothing of sinning and offending God. Our sins are like arrows being shot into the heavens and piercing the heart of God himself. He loves us so much mere words are unable to describe this kind of love. The pain we cause Him is beyond description. Unfathomable amounts of souls in despair could not match the sorrow He feels. God's love deserves more than we can give Him; should we not make an effort to at least try? His hands are holding back all His tears. His hands are holding back the wrath of heaven that we deserve. There are some devout Christians in this arena; unfortunately there are fewer and fewer as time goes on. Will you enter the arena with a heart open to God's love, or will you stay behind and break His heart? There is plenty of room if you choose to join me. Will you join me in this arena and accept God's love?

 The Visitor

One night, when I was entering the depth of prayer, a visitor entered my thoughts and began to speak to me. The voice was soft spoken and contained a false sense of love—I was uncertain if it was my imagination or real.
The voice began speaking to me: "There is no heaven, there is no hell, it is all part of your imagination, it is all a lie. Why do you believe in such foolishness?"
I answered the voice of my thoughts, "I do not know who you are...you are wrong!" The voice continued, "Why do you follow Jesus? What has He done for you? He ruined your life. Your good friends are gone. Many persecute and reject you. You are trying to be a Christian. Why would you waste your life for that? Do you know man made it all up? Why do you believe in such foolishness?"
As he was speaking, a darkness surrounded me. I felt the cold of this darkness pierce my body to the depth of my bones, and my teeth began to chatter. I could not shake the cold from my body, so I crawled under the blankets of my bed. I uttered these words: "Jesus is my strength! Jesus is my strength! Jesus is my strength!" The voice responded, "You do not have enough faith to rebuke me; you are still a child with so much to learn." He continued to torment me with his words. He said, "Who are you in comparison to me? I have entered the thoughts of many, starting with your church. I have corrupted many men throughout history including popes, bishops, and priests. I have divided Christians, created false religious beliefs, and thousands of different denominations of believers who claim to know the truth. I have created false prophets and misled millions far from God's truth. I have taught many to hate, cheat, and steal, putting brother against brother. I am the cause of wars, I was there for numerous plagues, famines, disasters, and diseases that resulted in millions of innocent lives lost. I am the master of destruction and death. You are nothing. I have reduced the truth and turned it into a lie. I created a world of nonbelievers, self seekers who are not interested in God and His church. "Again, I tried to rebuke him; I was afraid and doubt filled my soul. His voice turned to anger and he called me stupid. "I am Satan, ruler of this world! If you do not reject Jesus and return to the life you came from, I will make your life on this earth a living hell! I will turn your dreams into nightmares, your hope into despair, your peace into trouble. You will have no joy on this earth until the day you die. When you die, you will remain in the ground never to awaken again." In hesitation, I replied in return, "If what you are saying is true, then my new life in Jesus is a lie!" He replied, "Yes." I said, "No, because who I am and what I know denies what you say. My life in sin never brought me happiness—true happiness. I lived in moments and pockets of joy, never feeling complete. I also know what true love is, and the only person who can give me that love is God alone!" He replied, "You are such a fool! You will be rejected and hated by many. Even the church you love will reject you. Know this: I will torment you the rest of your life." The cold and the darkness left my body and soul upon Satan's departure. I know in my heart this is not the end of this encounter. I will trust in the Lord, my Rock and Savior.

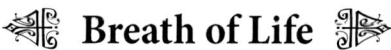 Breath of Life

You, Lord, are my breath of life from which I draw my life.

Before I knew You, I drew life from a world which many people draw from: surviving on the oxygen from a world of untruth, breathing in deception and sustaining life on false hopes and empty dreams which contain imaginary joys. They continue breathing in from an unclean source of contaminated air.

One day when I was searching for You, You breathed upon me and Your breath entered my lungs and began to purify my body and soul; it lasted only a moment. You allowed me to journey towards You, which felt like a lifetime. I was trying so hard to draw my breath from You, hoping You would be my only source of life. You allowed me to draw my breath from the world as well as a small breath from You. You were weaning me from the world where I had spent most of my life drawing the air of deception. I was unable to take a deep breath from You in fear that I might become prideful and foolish. I needed to know that I had to depend on You and less on myself. I might have lost direction from the incredible rush of Your love. At times, I felt that I would have died from the lack of Your spiritual oxygen. The world's oxygen was choking me and my lungs were filled with deception and lies, resulting in unwanted sin, causing me to feel a deep separation from You. I knew I had to cross the desert of suffering and temptations so that I would see how weak and frail I am without You. It was necessary to see and understand that, by myself, I would be vulnerable and easy prey for the Devil. He rejoices in our suffering and spends every minute of every day deceiving countless numbers of souls, causing them to sin and fall away from You. I cannot describe the joy I felt when Your breath first entered my lungs. I felt alive and clean. You allowed me to bathe in Your love through tiny little breaths. It felt like Heaven's doors were wide open, flooding my soul. Love, peace, and joy overwhelmed me while the world's breath paused for a brief moment. I was held in suspension by the breath of Heaven that swept me off my feet and allowed me to float high above the clouds in a place consumed by total love. You stripped my lungs of worldly oxygen and filled them with heavenly air.

Every so often, I catch a breath of the world's oxygen which passes through my lungs, causing me to sin. It saddens me, and at the same time, reminds me of how much I need You. I am constantly watching for the deceiver who sneaks his breath into all of us when we are not paying attention. When we least expect it, his breath enters our bodies fast, before we can even close our mouths.

Now I watch and breathe with caution, knowing that when I least expect it, the Devil will try to breathe his lies into me. I will praise Your name as the enemy is approaching me; he will be defeated because Your words are truth. I know, Lord, that You are the breath of life from which I need to draw life. Fill my lungs to capacity, setting me free from the world from which I have been drawing life. I want to continue drawing life from You: breathe into me.

 Armored

My son, you have been on a long journey for which I had to prepare you. Know there are many who came before you, and there will be many who will come after you. Sometimes it takes many years to form a child before he is ready to battle against evil in the world. Your life before you knew Me consisted of much sin: I can use a person's sinful nature and turn them into good. Before your conversion, you had a fighting spirit that you used for your own personal gain. I have taken that spirit and turned it around so you can battle for My purpose—the ultimate good of souls. I allowed you some time so you could see how sinful your life was before you came to know Me. It would have been too much for you to understand. I did not want you to fall into despair; the knowledge of who you really were would have been too much for you to bear. It can be compared to a flower that was exposed to the rain and nearly drowned. Expecting to bear the extreme heat of the desert sun, the flower would have dried up and withered away. I had to allow you to see your weaknesses and your sinfulness in your journey. By doing this, I knew you would show mercy to those who walked in your footsteps, being less judgmental and more compassionate to those around you who appeared to be lost and confused.

I breathed My life into your lungs and filled your mind with understanding and heavenly wisdom. I showed you My precepts and planted them deep inside your heart so you could bear the weight of the armor I encased you with. This armor will not protect your body; it will allow you to let go of it. It is the armor of My love. It will allow you to endure great suffering within your physical body for the love of others without concern for yourself. I have prepared your mind, heart, body, and soul for the road that lies ahead of you. I have placed, piece by piece, the armor necessary to protect you against the Devil in this spiritual battle. Even if you should die in the flesh, My love will protect your soul. I will not shield your eyes. It will be necessary for My light to enter you when you have fallen: I will pick you up. I will not cover your mouth because, when My spirit is in you, it will be necessary for you to speak the words I need spoken. Your nose will be exposed, as well, so that you can continue to breathe the air I will breathe into you to help sustain your life. The Devil will no longer be able to attack you from behind; he will now approach you from the front. You will have clear knowledge of his presence. You can no longer rely on your own senses—they will mislead you. Be cautious with your emotions: you cannot allow them to control your thoughts and decisions. Remain in prayer unceasingly. This will be necessary to sustain you when you do not feel My presence. It will be necessary to call upon My name when the Devil confronts you. Do not attempt to battle against him or any other demons without calling upon My name. You are armored with the spiritual gifts I have given you. They will help you to discern right from wrong, good from evil, and what is sinful in My eyes.

I am with you always. Do not be afraid. My truth is within you. It will guide you.

The Mountain

The Lord called me out of the desert where I stood at the edge. In front of me was a great wall not made of stone or anything solid. It was a dense fog through which I could not see. So I stood on the edge of the desert, afraid to go forward, uncertain what was ahead of me. I remembered that the Lord had shielded me with the armor of His love, protecting my soul from eternal damnation: I was still concerned of the possibility of physical assault. I waited on the Lord, hoping and praying He would arrive soon. As time went on, I grew tired and the Devil began his assault on my mind, creating fear and doubt within me. I fell to my knees and began to pray. I said, "Lord, I cannot do this; I am just a simple man. There are many that are wiser, more prayerful, devout, and holier than I. Why me, Lord? I am just a miserable sinner who is unable to do anything without Your grace, mercy, and love." Then I picked up my head and looked into the dense fog. I could see a light approaching me: it stopped a distance from me. I was unable to see who or what was approaching. Then a voice spoke from within the fog and said to me, "My son, why do you doubt Me? You rely too much on your senses. I want you to put your doubt aside and follow Me." I proceeded forward as if I were blindfolded. I could feel the incline under my feet and I felt I was walking for days. The voice remained silent the whole time, and I remained obedient to that voice. I finally reached the peak of a high mountain. I could not see beyond the clouds below me. I sat on the peak of that mountain trying to look beyond the clouds below me, unable to see anyone or hear anyone's voice. Then a hand reached out from the heavens and touched me on my forehead. My body began to burn with the love of God inside me. I felt my body leaving the ground and ascending to the heavens. I was soaring with angels. Then I saw the Lord before me. I turned my head away from Him in fear and shame. He said to me, "Do not be afraid. I know all of your sins. You are not here to be judged. I am sending you out like a fox among wolves. You must rely on heavenly wisdom in your battle against evil. You will live on the spiritual highs of the mountains and the spiritual lows of the valleys. You will have moments where you will feel alone; you will have moments where My love will consume you. You will sore on eagles' wings like an angel in flight through the heavens, high above the earth were no one can touch you or cause you any harm. Go now, there is much for you to do." I felt the hand of the Lord let me go and I began to plunge towards the earth. I passed through the clouds and continued to descend downward, closing my eyes in fear. Then the hand of the Lord reached out and caught me. He gently put me on the ground and said to me, "My son, if the sun never shined and darkness filled the sky, you would have the moon and the stars for light. So it is with me. Even when it seems that My light is not shining bright like the sun, I will be your moon and stars. I will always be your light. You will never walk in the darkness again."

Final Preparation

The Lord sat me down in a new valley to reflect and meditate. It was not like the old valley or desert that I had experienced, where I felt so vulnerable and fell into despair and doubt. In this valley I drew all my strength from Jesus, and not myself. I never felt alone. I knew deep within, Jesus would always be with me. While sitting on the ground, I looked all around me at all of God's creation and saw the beauty in it. I started to understand that in the past I was always looking outside the picture that God wanted me to focus on—the picture I had painted inside myself. As I continued looking through my own eyes, as if I were standing in front of a mirror looking inside myself, I began to reflect on the picture that I had painted and my heart became saddened. I knew it was not the picture that God had painted for me. The Lord wanted me to reflect on my past. I saw the early stages of my Christian life. A self-proclaimed Christian. I saw the foundation I had built on sand, supported by self-love and pride. I was unable to see the depth of these sins inside me. I then passed the surface of my interior and saw my desires and the sinfulness of them. I did not like the way I felt when I confronted them.

My body and emotions were being controlled by the desires of my flesh. So I continued to go deeper within myself and entered my thoughts. I saw my thoughts controlling my desires. So I said to myself, "If I can control my thoughts, then I can control my desires," not realizing that my thoughts were controlled by other sources. I needed to confront them before I could achieve the understanding necessary to serve the Lord. So I continued towards the basement of my soul to see what I had accumulated during the course of my life. I saw the sins of my life deep within my soul; they were hidden from my conscience making it impossible to see them in my everyday life. My sins were like branches drawing life from a tree whose roots were planted deep in the ground. My roots were planted in darkness and not in the light of Christ. I realized I had indulged in so many sinful things that had brought me pleasure and, what I thought was beauty, only to be blinded by the roots supplying the poison to my soul. Drawing life from the roots of darkness, I was slowly dying from within. I finally reached the basement of my soul and used the light of Christ to see what was hidden inside myself. I saw my sins emitting rays of darkness to my thoughts, which in turn emitted their rays to my desires. I watched my body respond to them. Then I saw the core that emitted rays to the sins that were above it. I drew closer to it, and saw its roots embedded in my soul as it continued to emit rays. God wanted me to know this creature deep within me. It would be the cause of my downfall and separation from God. I turned my face in shame, afraid to confront it. It was my pride which stood before me, rooted in the depth of my soul. My greatest sin which gave life to all my other sins. The source of all my suffering and the hardships I had endured throughout my life. I knew I would have to uproot this deadly sin before I could go on: that humility would be the only tool I would have in uprooting and defeating this enemy. I knew in my heart if I did not defeat it, it would defeat me.

 Prideful

You, Lord, are my light, my strength, my everything. Out of each breath I will praise Your name, for Your breath is life that will last forever. Your light is constantly shining on me, exposing the darkness within my soul, revealing to me what is within me. Sometimes I am too blind to see my own sinfulness. I did not see the pride that planted its roots in the dark side of my soul. An enemy entered into me without my knowledge, like a seed that entered the earth, falling to the ground without notice of its existence. I foolishly watered it and it started to grow, my actions providing it with all the nutrients necessary and nourished by the people I competed with for worldly power and possession. I also felt the need to defend myself in order to protect the image of who I wanted them to see. I know You are constantly revealing to me the errors of my ways. It is only through true humility that I will be able to battle and defend Your truth. Give me the strength when I am in the heat of persecution to remain silent, submissive, and obedient when others breathe words of hatred and disrespect upon me. Let me only open my mouth to defend Your truth, out of love for my fellow brothers and sisters, and not in the defense of myself.

And those who speak poorly of me—those who slander my name because of my love for You and Your Church—let the pain of their insults never pierce my soul. Give me the understanding necessary to realize the only opinion I should concern myself with would be Yours, knowing in my heart that the opinion of others will not get me through Heaven's doors. And when the poor come across my path, let me embrace them with pity, mercy, and love, knowing in my heart that we are all equal in Your eyes. And when the rich, who might be lost in their own wealth and pride, arrive, let me not be envious of what they possess for fear of losing what I possess in You, knowing You are the greatest treasure, far exceeding any material thing. I realize they may disparage me because I have fewer things than they do. Let me embrace those who think I am foolish because I choose to embrace Your love and follow You, knowing they do not understand my heart or the love I possess for Your ways and truth.

Lord, reduce me to nothing so that everything and everyone is above me. Let me be a servant that You will find pleasing in Your eyes. Let me never speak a word in my defense to protect my name in the world of names, written in a book by the master deceiver who caused the world to be filled with pride, self-love, and the desire for possessions. He has recorded many names with no concern, love, or need of those he enslaved by their passions. They are recorded in the book of eternal damnation, taken from You so that he can possess them for himself for all of eternity. Poor lost souls.

I know my pride keeps me from knowing You and a deeper union with You. Allow me to no longer bathe in the waters of pride; I do not want to live in fear of drowning in pride. Take my hand, pull me from these waters, and save me.

Table of Knights

The Lord then showed me the table of knights. It was not like any other table I had ever seen. It could not be understood by the human mind. It was a table that existed in the will of God where we are called to gather and unite with Him to merge our wills to His, forming an unbreakable chain of love and faith to help the world of lost souls. This place consisted of many believers of all faiths. I saw walls of separation that were caused by the stubbornness and pride that existed in some believers who thought they were the possessors of the truth.

But the truth was shallow inside them. It was not deeply rooted and stood on a foundation built in the sands of the shifting earth, without a sound foundation to build upon. Many gathered at this spiritual table waiting for the Word of God to speak to them. We were surrounded by the forces of good and evil. Those who gathered at this table could be enlightened or deceived. There were many so-called truths that some believers claimed to be the truth, yet were far from the truth.

Both Heaven and Hell were breathing their spirit upon all who sat at the table, causing confusion among the weaker in faith. They were unable to discern the lies the Devil was breathing upon them, not knowing they were being overtaken by these lies permeating their souls. It clouded their thinking, making it impossible for them to see the truth and would leave them vulnerable when the time came to enter the battlefield on the road to Heaven. It is hard to describe what entered my mind as I sat at this table surrounded by fellow Christians:

I was concerned, saddened, and disappointed. I knew in the depth of my soul many were going to fall away from God and back into the world. Heaven was on the other side of the battlefield. We had a long fight ahead of us in this war on the spiritual battlefield. Many Christians appeared to claim to possess something that was still too far out of reach, trying to secure the very thing that only God could give them. I knew in my heart the truth was not in them. Then I saw another group of Christians who believed God was inside them, thinking they did not need any churches or organized religions. I feared the strength of the Devil's breath as he continued breathing his lies on these knights, whose armor he easily penetrated as he entered their souls, misleading them. I began to doubt and was concerned about my own soul, wondering if the armor I wore would withstand the assaults that were ahead of me on this spiritual battlefield. I reflected on the thoughts of God and remembered what He had taught me and how He was always there even when I could not feel Him next to me. I knew in my heart that He had brought me this far and that He would carry me through to the end. The Lord had shown me this table of knights not to discourage me, but to strengthen me.

I know that His truth will get me across the battlefield as I battle against sin. We live in a world that is constantly trying to redefine the truth. We all have our own beliefs. It will now be a matter of whose beliefs will get across the battlefield to the gates of Heaven.

Friendship

On this earth, we would find it difficult to persevere without a good friend by our side. Our Lord, will always be our best friend and should never come second to anyone. I have found it difficult, at times, when I need someone to talk with, to rely on the Lord alone. There have been times when He does not seem to answer me. That is why the Lord has given us friends. I always hope and pray that He sends me good friends. God did not create people to be bad; it is the desires of our hearts that changes us and turns us into something that is not appealing.

In the Christian journey, it is more difficult to find friends that are true to God and His ways. I want you to know in my journey these many years, my heart has been broken several times. I have often been blinded, desiring to find someone who would love the Lord with all their heart, mind, body and soul. I also realize I have failed to love Him as I should. I expect too much from my friends; I should expect less from them and more from myself and be an example of God's love. You, Lord, are my best friend. I can always count on You even when You are not there.

I will always let You down because I let my desires carry me away on the sweeping winds of worldly desires and foolish dreams: like the winds in a storm that carry things away only to deposit them somewhere down the road, never to be found again. I let my love for You be swept away by foolish things, temporary things, prizes which cannot be held. How many times I let them slip away like treasures that turn to dust and fade away! Earthly treasures, how temporary you truly are!

Good friends last forever. They are not like possessions that can be bought and sold. You can count on them when the storms of life are pounding on you and the bottom of your world appears to have fallen out. They will stretch out their hands and save you from falling into the world of darkness and despair. Good friends are like building blocks that build upon each other, forming an unbreakable wall.

In the Christian world, we help each other in our battle against sin. We act as a support system, constantly encouraging one another in our personal battles against evil and sin in our own lives. Without God's grace we are so vulnerable. As much as we encourage one another, without His grace we will fall.

As friends, we know each other's weaknesses and try to offer support. As I am preparing to enter the spiritual battlefield, I fear for my friend more than myself. Not that I am better than her, because I am not. I have spent much time helping her to understand and battle against her weaknesses.

Her desires are too strong and her faith is too weak. She struggles with prayer and puts her faith in the title of being a Catholic. She justifies her actions and many times has misunderstood her blessings because of her lack of understanding of the suffering that comes with the cross. My friend, I will pray for you, and please pray for me as we enter the battlefield for Jesus. Know that I love you. I will try to be there when you need me. When you fall, I will reach out to you, and if you should turn your back on me, I will never stop loving you. You will always be a part of me. May our Lord comfort and bless you always.

Amen.

The Walk

As my friend and I headed towards the spiritual battlefield as soldiers for Christ, my heart weighed heavily. I knew in my heart that I was a sinner and always will be as long as I am on this earth. I grew tired of letting Jesus down—feeling like a disappointment to all of Heaven, ashamed of my weaknesses and sinfulness. I felt as if all of Heaven was looking down upon me. I wanted them to believe in me. I hoped that they understood me. I could not help myself from thinking how brave and strong they were in defending God's truth. How powerful their preaching to the world was about His love and mercy. Their hearts and souls were so strong in Christ, their love for Him so intense. How could I compare to that? I began to doubt my own strength in Him. I knew the strength of the Devil and how he has manipulated millions of innocent people, turning them from God. I knew this master of lies would always be near me, waiting for the opportunity to deceive me and cause me to sin. I also feared for my friend whom I dearly loved. It was not that I did not trust in the Lord, because I did trust in Him. It was because my mind wandered at times, and in that moment the Devil would enter, causing me to sin against our Lord whom I love and did not want to offend.

In my journey, I have come across many different kinds of Christians, who in their arrogance and their blindness, fail to understand and see the truth of the spiritual battlefield. Blinded by deception, they have formed illusions of being the ultimate warriors for Christ. In their closed-mindedness, they were too ignorant to understand the actual reality of this war. They put up a front as if nothing could defeat them inside; they are broken, confused, and all alone in need of God's comfort. They claim to cast out demons yet fail to face the demons in the closet of their own souls, struggling with their own sinfulness, broken limbs from the tree of life. Their lack of humility leaves them blinded and vulnerable to the assaults of the Devil, tossing them across the battlefield like weightless objects in the wind, like leaves being stomped on by the weight of sin unable to get up and fly again.

Both my friend and I still lack true humility, leaving us vulnerable, too.

I pray for the understanding of my own sinfulness and my lack of humility; that He will give me a greater understanding of what will be necessary to battle for Him. That when I enter this battlefield I do not enter with my own strength, but in Him who is my strength—my only hope for survival. That I am not foolish enough to think that I can do this on my own. That my love for Christ is stronger than my love of myself. In my love for Jesus, I can be the person who will not hesitate to sacrifice my life for my friend. In my heart, mind, and soul, let my only concern be the salvation of my friend, myself, and all the others that will be on this battlefield. May I never forget Your ultimate sacrifice on the cross, Lord. Strip me naked, take my hands and feet, and nail them to the cross with You. Pierce my side and let me die with You. I am an unworthy child; pour out Your mercy and love upon me. Please let me be like a son to You. Let me die for You.

 Baptism

As I drew closer to the spiritual battlefield, I found myself going back in time to my baptism, knowing that some Christians think being baptized as a child is foolish and unnecessary. So I reflected upon a ritual that took place many years ago when I was a child in the arms of my mother, wrapped in white signifying purity. At the altar, I awaited the outpouring of holy water upon my head while my eyes looked towards the heavens, surrounded by the people that were to raise me in the faith. They were to be my teachers, guiding me and helping me to understand the truth. It was my parents' beliefs that allowed this ritual to take place. The water was poured upon my head initiating the first installment of the heavenly promises and receiving the most exceptional gift of life ever promised to a human being. I received the spirit of God within me as a person receives a blood transfusion in order to be saved from dying. I received the living Spirit of God, along with His spiritual gifts, that were planted deep within my soul, unaware of their existence. His spirit and His spiritual gifts would remain undiscovered within me until His appointed hour like treasures placed in a chest of life, waiting patiently for the Spirit inside me to open them. The Spirit laid unnoticed inside me for many years. These treasures were buried deep within my soul, awaiting God's grace to open them. They remained hidden within my soul until the day when God awakened me from my slumber and freed me from my worldliness and selfishness. Once awakened by God's grace, I began searching, trying to mature in spirit and attempting to bring His gifts to their full potential. At that same moment in time, when the water was being poured upon my head, I was also being cleansed free from the world that could take me from Him. Only for a brief moment in time, the evil one could not harm me. He stood and watched the Holy Spirit enter into me, waiting for his moment when he could turn me away from Him. No human eye could see beyond the water's contents. I had no understanding of its power and its strength as it was entering my soul. It appeared to everyone like water washing down my face, but there was more than they could see; much more. In that moment of baptism, the Spirit of God was purifying my mind, heart, and soul. It infused my mind with the knowledge of His Spirit deep in my consciousness, like a seed planted deep into the earth, waiting for the rains and the sun to bring life to it. In time, God's grace would bring life to my soul, flooding it with the things of God and purifying me. The knowledge of God dwells deep in everyone's consciousness: He can be found within all of us. We are joined to Him through baptism, becoming part of Him, and receiving from Him everything He ever wanted us to have. It appears to be a mystery to many who might remain blinded all their lives. I was once blind and now I can see. I was baptized, brought to life, and given new hope and strength in the heavenly promise and the gift of eternal life. All of this was made possible through the gateway of the rushing waters that were poured upon my head: the day of my baptism when water and Spirit flowed on and through me.

Penance

Such an important sacrament, misunderstood by many, leaving them lost and empty. There are those who believe that they can confess to Jesus directly and be forgiven—maybe so. But is the forgiveness on the surface only, never piercing the depth of the soul? Never truly feeling forgiven because they never hear the words of absolution—necessary in true forgiveness? If the apostles, guided by the Holy Spirit, could speak the words necessary to move so many to Christ, then is it possible that God could deliver His words through one priest to one sinner? Can the Holy Spirit enter through the mouth of an individual who, in an imperfect state, does not use his own words, but the words of the Holy Spirit spoken through him? Through Confession, the soul that humbles itself before God and man could receive graces, helping one to understand the depth of one's sinfulness. In humility the doorway to a soul opens up, emptying out one's sins before God and man, leaving sins at the doorway, allowing room for God's graces to enter the room of their soul, and filling it with the mercy of Jesus's love. In our arrogance, do we refuse to admit our sins and failings, only to succumb to the Devil's call to feed on us and fall short of receiving God's grace?

There are those who believe all sins are equal in the harm they cause the soul. They believe no sin is greater than another and they do not believe in mortal or venial sins. I tell you some sins are more mortal or fatal to your soul than others because they consume your heart with great strength, dividing your love between God and yourself and taking from God what is rightfully His—your love. This fatal attraction will tear your heart and soul to pieces, leaving you in a state of incompleteness and making you unable to receive the pure love set aside for you. The love inside you becomes contaminated with self-love and the soul will continue to plunge into the dark murky waters of evil making it impossible to bathe in the waters of eternal life. In Confession, you need to know and understand that we all struggle, including our priests. You may feel in your heart that the priest may never understand your weaknesses or anything about you. You may be concerned about what he will think of you. If you enter Confession for the wrong reasons, you will receive the wrong answers and will not feel the forgiveness of Jesus. Nothing should remain hidden from the priest, because it is not hidden from God. It will remain a mystery to some who will fail to understand the forgiveness available to the sincere of heart. Beyond the curtain between an individual and the priest, there stands a mediator between the individual and God: an instrument of God's forgiveness spoken through the mouth of a man and received by the soul in need of forgiveness. This allows God's grace to shower upon them and cleanse them, freeing them from the weight and suffering of their sins. Enter Confession with true humility, knowing you are a sinner and expecting to hear the words of Jesus through the priest who speaks them to you. And when you leave, know you are forgiven. For the kingdom of God is given to those who truly believe.

Communion

My first encounter with the spiritual food sent from Heaven was when I was a young boy. It came after I received the Sacrament of Penance which cleared an area within my soul that awaited the foundation to be set: the structure of which only God could build upon. I had to receive the Lord in a state of grace. It was when I reached manhood that I began to defile my Lord through my sinful thoughts and actions. Although as a child I did not fully comprehend the true mysteries of Communion due to my immaturity and lack of understanding, I did finally receive Jesus for the first time and the foundation was laid within my soul. Although I was still unaware of this powerful encounter with our Lord, I did receive Him into my soul. Like so many of us, after the foundation of our Lord is set, we walk away. I walked away and journeyed through my Catholic faith through my teen years to manhood, walking around spiritually blind with no interest in a union with our Lord. I had no knowledge of the foundation in my soul that laid dormant awaiting the arrival of spiritual lumber to be set upon it. I spent the majority of my life buying and collecting unfit lumber not worthy to be set on that foundation. My sins and my desires purchased material unfit to be laid upon and, in time, mortal sin would burn inside me, destroying all that was purchased and leaving only a foundation with no building to protect me from the world of darkness. I had no place to call home, just an empty cellar hole. Then the grace of God saved me and drew me back to His Church. All I had with me was a suitcase of filth which contained the sins of my life that were never confessed. I brought the suitcase into the confessional and, dumping all of its contents upon the ground, I asked for forgiveness and received absolution. I left a free man; I now was able to receive our Lord in a state of grace.

Over time, through frequent communion with our Lord through the Eucharist, and Confessions, I began collecting the lumber necessary to build my house. I use the Sacraments and the virtues as the tools necessary to build my house. Through Confession and Communion, I am building a house so strong that, in time, the evil one will not be able to enter and destroy what I have built in union with God.

Through Communion I receive our Lord—His body which was offered up and sacrificed for me, providing real food sent from Heaven to feed my soul. There is something beyond the Host which becomes the Body of Christ; something beyond our senses in the world of the supernatural. Transubstantiation is a mystery to many of us who still might be blinded because of lack of understanding or love for God. There you will find your encounter with Jesus. Move past your senses, close your eyes, open your heart and soul, open your mouth, and in a state of grace let Jesus enter into you. Let Him search your heart, fill your veins, and flow through your body with His everlasting love. Let His love consume you and overflow from you. Your communion with Jesus is the only Communion that can set you free; there is no other communion that can do this.

 Confirmation

I was a teenager, immature and unaware of the gifts I was going to receive in the Sacrament of Confirmation: the gifts that only the Holy Spirit could give me. I was not alone—many of my classmates were unprepared to receive His gifts as well. We were taught by our teachers about His power within us. Unfortunately, at the time of our Confirmation, the world had already consumed our hearts; our minds were not focused on the Holy Spirit, but on the things of the world.

We were temples that should have been filled with the things of God, but because we rejected His ways, we became temples of earthen vessels. The day came when we were to confirm the Holy Spirit within us. Our class entered the church along with classes from other Catholic churches. We waited for the bishop to call upon the Spirit of the Lord to be awakened within us, similar to the Pentecost.

I stood and waited as the many before me walked forward to call upon the Holy Spirit within them. As I waited, I stood bored, hoping for my turn to arrive and for the celebration to end. My turn arrived, and I proceeded forward, standing before the bishop who would call upon this mysterious guest that was within me, who the Church felt was necessary for me to know. I looked into the bishop's eyes as he raised his hand over my head and began to pray. I stood there patiently, nervously awaiting some great miracle to awaken my body and soul and, without my knowledge, the Holy Spirit within me began looking for an opening inside my darkened soul. The door of my soul was opened by the calling of the bishop through the Sacrament of Confirmation. The Holy Spirit, finding an opening in my soul, entered deeper and looking around, found no temple worthy of such a guest. Nothing was prepared for His arrival, there was no place for Him to rest, and finding no place to rest, no place to call home, hid in a faraway place within me, saddened by what He saw. He then took one last look at the foundation laid within me many years ago by the Sacraments I had received earlier in my life.

He circled the foundation finding that it was strong because it was built upon the sacraments of Baptism, Penance, and Communion. He decided to leave some additional spiritual gifts inside the foundation of my soul, awaiting the day for the gifts to come to life within me. These would be necessary to build the temple of the Lord within my body, giving life to the body which was dying because of sin. The Holy Spirit then looked towards Heaven saddened. He remained unnoticed for there was nothing more He could do. The Devil, seeing the Spirit unnoticed, moved towards the gifts that were left behind and covered them with his darkness, hoping I would never find them and open them. They would remain covered inside the foundation of my soul for many years, inside my darkened soul, awaiting the light of Christ to shine upon them for me to see.

I was blind at the time of Confirmation, a foolish young man. However, even my blindness did not keep the Holy Spirit from descending deeper into my soul and leaving His additional gifts behind which I opened later in my life on the day of my conversion.

 Marriage

You, Oh Lord, created marriage, bonding man and woman together in union with each other and with You. For that which is created sacred is beautiful in its sacredness. In that union, the love for You was to be built, taking two individuals who were to love You completely, uniting their love for You, and building upon it through You. They were to put their trust in You first, then that trust would move them to build their trust in each other, allowing them to completely trust in You for each other's well-being. Upon this rock, they would build the foundation of their spiritual household. Within this household, the two, now one, would grow in sacrificial love, the avenue necessary for a deeper intimacy with You. You may choose to bless them with children, knowing what is best for them. They were to raise their children in the love of God, the source of true love. The world was to multiply and grow in love for You. The man was to love his wife as his equal because he knew how to love You. He was to be the guardian of his wife and family, providing for their needs and protecting them from harm, for You gave him great physical strength. The woman was to love her husband and trust in him, as she trusted in God to guide him. The woman became the vessel necessary to carry children; but not only that, also a heart capable of carrying unending love, reflecting Your love for all mankind. Together they would contain Your love, Your strength, Your mercy, and Your justice. The Devil saw this, and hated this because he hates anything and anyone that contains You. He saw the woman as a key to the family as he saw Eve the key to the fall of mankind—away from You. He entered the minds of certain women who were weak in faith and made them vessels of seduction, seducing men who were weak in faith as well. Selfishness entered and the marriage began to be rewritten. The Devil was pleased, but not content. He decided to rewrite the woman as an individual, who should be independent of man, as a competitor to man. The Devil was pleased with what he saw, but was still dissatisfied. He decided to corrupt the offspring and turn them away from God. The two that remained together in marriage, remained together as individuals, separated from God. They became materialistic and gave their children the materialistic world, and the family fell away from God. The Devil was still dissatisfied with the family divided. He entered the minds of the offspring, allowing them to feel entitled to everything, convincing them that the parents owed them. He divided what God united. The knowledge of God then left the family, and His love departed with it, because they chose to love themselves over Him. The world, in its individualism, is unable to embrace the love of God, leaving families crippled and broken. They continue to enslave themselves to their passions and false hopes. They grow in pride, self-love, and instant gratification, unable to be satisfied. They are jealous, hating anyone who possesses something they do not. Marriage is, and always will be, an avenue to grow in love. Those who use this Sacrament wisely will know love.

Behold

The Lord:

Behold before your eyes the suffering My Son endured for the sins of the world. He was like a beautiful flower that blossomed upon the earth, then was trampled upon by the weight of the sins of mankind—your sins and those of the whole world. Open your eyes and behold His suffering. Open your heart and feel His pain. Strip yourself naked and embrace His scourging, for your hour has come to give witness to the truth.

The Servant:

My eyes were opened as I stood watching the passion of our Lord. I stood in shame as I beheld His suffering. I saw Judas walking towards our Lord as he was about to kiss Him. Then saw myself kissing our Lord with the kiss of betrayal. I saw the apostles fleeing from the garden, and I was fleeing with them in fear of my life, afraid of defending the truth, for the truth was not strong enough within me. Then I stood with Peter in the courtyard as the people accused us of being His followers. We denied Him three times, then we fell to our knees in shame. I watched them take Him away to be scourged. I saw myself whipping Him and beating Him, sometimes tearing His flesh away from His body, and feeling no remorse. I watched Him trying to hold Himself up as I continued to whip Him, and I watched the weight of sin continue the fall upon His shoulders, slowly bringing Him to His knees. Then I placed the crown of thorns upon His head, pushing as hard as I could, causing Him severe pain as I saw my sins within the thorns. I gave Him His cross and told Him to carry it, which He did with great joy. Then I laid Him upon the cross and drove the nails into His hands and feet causing Him severe pain, which He endured for the love of the human race. I picked Him up while nailed to the cross and stood Him before the world, between two sinners, and put Him to shame. And in the end, I pierced Him as blood and water started pouring upon my head. Then my Lord looked upon me and said:

The Lord:

Because of your sins, and the sins of the world, I endured this suffering. Let the blood and water that rush forth from My pierced body cleanse and renew you. Let my spirit dwell within you, giving testimony to the truth. I allowed you to crucify Me in hopes that you would understand. I still stand crucified by a world that still rejects Me, which truly does not understand Me. I was crucified in the flesh by the hands of men. I still stand condemned and crucified by the hearts of a lost world.

 The Battlefield

We finally arrived at the battlefield. There were hundreds of us who were prepared by the Holy Spirit to do battle against the evil forces of this world. The Holy Spirit continued filling our minds with understanding and with spiritual gifts needed in the hope that we would be prepared for our encounter with the forces of evil. I personally was carrying with me the graces I had received through the Sacraments along with the graces I had received throughout my life. Also, graces given to me through my conversion with the power of prayer, and I carried with me the sword of truth. I knew in my heart that the wisdom God had given me would not be enough to carry me through this journey. I had to put my faith in God and the prayer life that I had established, realizing that I would fall into temptation. I also had to accept my nothingness in the hope that God, seeing my humility, would show me mercy by pouring His graces upon me, allowing me to get back up on my feet and fight with the stronger spirit which would be necessary to reach the goal at the end of the battlefield known as Heaven. We stood and looked at each other, awaiting the arrival of an angel of the Lord to instruct us. My heart became saddened as I looked into the eyes of some of those around me who, with confidence in themselves, expected to enter this battlefield and not be defeated. I realized that their pride would come before their fall and blindness had filled their souls. I became concerned about my own soul's well-being. The angel of the Lord finally arrived and greeted us, saying to us, "Welcome children of the Lord! May God's grace be upon you." In return, we greeted the angel. The angel then spoke again to us. "The Lord has planted His spirit within you and has given you certain gifts necessary for the battle ahead of you. Do not enter the field alone, but rely on each other, draw strength from each other's gifts, and through prayer and the grace of God. He has given you wisdom so that you should not be deceived. Use it wisely in the face of temptation and pray hard when temptation comes your way, for you will fall if you rely on yourself and your own strength. Do not become overconfident: let humility be the sword you use to defeat your enemy. And, when you fall, know that the weakness is within you and not your Lord and God who is your strength. Do not curse His name when the hammer of evil is pounding upon you. He allows this to humble you so that you will call upon His name in time of need. Every suffering is a blessing and every blessing is endured through the fires of humility. Pride endures nothing and rebels against all things that come against it. Many of you will fall and will not get back up, for the temptations will consume your heart and soul. You allow them to consume you because you close your eyes to the truth that is within you. Enter the battlefield at will, and may God's mercy and grace be with you. Pray always and carry with you the sword of truth and humility." The angel departed, and we knew what we had to do. I was concerned for my dear friend next to me and for myself, yet I knew in my heart that the Lord would not abandon me to the netherworld—to be eternally damned from Him.

The Spirits

We proceeded onto the battlefield and had walked only a few steps when we were greeted by two spirits. We stood in shock and awe as they stood before us. They were enormous in size and we were unable to see beyond them. All the warriors for the Lord began to look at each other and started to tremble, uncertain of what these spirits were, or what they wanted from us. They stood side-by-side looking at us—one was much larger than the other. Then, out of nowhere, one of the warriors spoke up and shouted at the spirits, "We are the warriors of the Lord, identify yourselves to us!" He also said, "The Lord will protect us against you." The larger one spoke to him and said, "Be silent, foolish one, for out of the mouths of fools are the words that lead to their destruction. Know your enemy's strength before you choose to battle against them, because within you are many weaknesses that you are blinded to. They will lead to your destruction." Then the smaller spirit spoke. "Wise men do not test the Spirit of the Lord within them, but will beseech the Lord in the spirit of humility. I am the spirit of truth and next to me is the spirit of untruth, we are hidden in the hearts and souls of all mankind. Within every thought that enters the human mind, one must choose what is truth and what is untruth. We stand before you and are within you. We will be there until the day you die. You will be greeted by many spirits in this world, each containing the truth and the untruth within them. The truth and the untruth that is within them will be revealed to you. You will have to choose one: choose wisely. I will allow the spirit of untruth to speak first so that you will know him." "I am the spirit of untruth, and within me are the desires of this world. Within my thoughts are the power of suggestions and manipulations leading to the inner desires of an individual's selfish and independent nature. Your flesh will desire me because I am desirable in many shapes and forms. I will corrupt your thoughts so that you do not desire to know or to live in the truth. I will leave you empty and blinded to its reality. And, I will make the road of truth undesirable to your flesh. I am the enemy of truth. I will imprison your soul, making the truth appear to be a lie so that you think your suffering comes from living in the truth." Then the spirit of truth spoke to us. "I am the spirit of truth, and though smaller in this world, I still remain the strongest and most rewarding. Only in the truth can a person truly be free and in that freedom can a person truly be happy. It is true that I am not desired by many because people think I come with great suffering in this world. I am not considered a reward in this life, but I am a reward in the next. Within me is the love of God and I am within Him. Anyone outside of us will feel the emptiness of the untruth within themselves. No one can live without the truth and feel complete in this life or in the next. It appears that I have very little to offer in this world, for worldly pleasures may keep you from finding me. I will never deceive you, or lead you astray. You will never feel the emptiness of the untruth within you if you choose me. Within me is the most important thing you should ever desire: the guarantee of eternal life in paradise."

The Unending Battle

The spirits of truth and untruth departed and the spirit within moved me to find a place of solitude because my heart weighed heavy. I found a cross on the battlefield that was unoccupied, without an owner. There was something unusual about the cross, drawing me to it. Then I stood underneath it and a voice spoke to me saying, "There are many crosses in this life which I have given, and will continue to give, but this cross I have reserved for the few. It comes with the spiritual eyes of Heaven, allowing you to see a glimpse of the world as I see it. It allows you to look deep within, beyond the external, not at a soul in its sinfulness, but in its emptiness. Your vision will not be limited to the lost and fallen away. I will also allow your vision to see the religious educators and shepherds of the Church as they really are, when I so will it. You will have moments of despair, and at times feel helpless and unwanted, sometimes feeling abandoned and alone. Do not lose hope: in these moments you will desire a deeper union with Me. Unfortunately, history repeats itself because mankind continues to repeat its sinfulness, so I will continue to send prophets as the world continues to reject them. Go now to My church and I will guide you." I picked up my cross and continued walking the battlefield of life, known as the spiritual battlefield. There were many truths and untruths on the battlefield that I was to battle, and would continue to battle. My close friend was defeated by the spirit of lust. She was deceived, compromised her faith, and left her husband for another man. When we first met, she listened to my advice with great joy, but later turned against me when I begged her to remain faithful to the Church's teachings and her husband. It was a great loss to me, but I continued forward. I was now faced with a bigger enemy. The deceiver had entered the hearts of many within the churches, both Protestant and Catholic. The churches were under attack, inside and out; the spirit of untruth was evident. My heart belongs to the Catholic church. I was exposed to the bitterness of fallen-away Catholics. In their pride and hatred towards the Church, they verbally assaulted me and the Church. I also was exposed to some of the religious educators and shepherds of our Holy Church who were being manipulated by the master of deception. They lived worldly lives and formed their own thoughts and opinions in contradiction to the Church's teachings. Pride ran rampant and their minds were closed. I was facing the creatures of falsehood, unable to break through their walls. I was nothing in the eyes of these religious leaders, like the many who came before me, hoping to shed light in the darkened areas of the Church. I began to question myself and felt God was wrong to expect so much from me. I knew in my heart I was wrong for doubting Him and His ways. My heart weighed heavily like a tree after a powerful snowstorm. I was leaning towards the ground waiting for the sun to rise and melt my sorrows away. Then I realized that the light of Christ and the torch of truth was, and is, my weapon against a world of darkness and the nails of untruth. I knew that darkness always gives way to the light and, in the end, God's light will prevail, darkness will be defeated, and my vision will only embrace the beauty of God's light.

 The Broken Covenant

Marriage is something more than the joining of a male and a female. It is a covenant between God, a man, and a woman. A covenant is not a commandment. It consists of an agreement between God and those He establishes the covenant with. In a covenant, He promises to remain faithful, even if those He establishes the covenant with do not. It is not like a contract between two parties where, if one party breaks their end of the agreement, the contract becomes void. No! God will remain faithful to His promise, regardless of whether we do, or not. "God created man in His image; in the divine image He created him; male and female He created them." (Genesis 1:27) God is truth and love. His truth and love live within us because we are created in His image. Next, the Bible describes the union between man and woman: "That is why a man leaves his father and mother and clings to his wife, and the two of them become one body." (Genesis 2:24). They become one body through the love of God, establishing a Trinity in love. The Trinity begins with the love of God for the man and woman. Second, the man and woman in this Trinity should choose to love God. In completing this Trinity, man and woman choose to love each other. This forms a three-way love and union within it. In his first letter to the Corinthians, St. Paul gives us an understanding of the defilement of this union, as well as sins of the body. "Avoid immorality. Every other sin a person commits is outside the body, but the immoral person sins against his own body. Do you not know that your body is a temple of the Holy Spirit within you, whom you have from God, and that you are not your own?" (1 Corinthians 6:18-19). In these verses, I see something sacred about the body, something stronger than the air we breathe. How do we perceive adultery? Our faith teaches that if we commit adultery, are truly sorry, and confess our sin in confession, we are forgiven. We are not required to tell our spouse or to ask him or her for forgiveness. I personally believe that a marriage is established in truth and love and it is possible to share with our best friend our weaknesses. Unfortunately, we do not live in a perfect world of forgiveness. We may choose to hide the sin from our spouses in order to protect them. The reality is every one of us is a sinner. Many of us are unable to handle the truth. Unfortunately, the sin which was forgiven in Confession may still remain hidden from the second person in this Trinity of love. Weak moments in time cannot be rewritten and families may be broken up because of divorce, with the possibility of losing everything. Many of us cannot understand human weakness, and betrayal cuts deep, making it impossible for a spouse to forgive us. Now we are forced to hide the truth from them? How nice it would be to be forgiven by both God and our spouse. No untruth in the marriage. A covenant unbroken. One heart, body, and soul in a Trinity of love. As humans, we make many decisions and choices, choosing between truth and untruth, free or imprisoned by the choices we make. It is not easy, and it never will be. In an almost perfect world, the conscience and the spirit can live in harmony with God and truly be happy.

 Sin

You are well disguised in a blanket of deception, hidden from the eyes of the innocent, who unknowingly welcomed you into their lives. You were born of the master of lies who manipulated our hearts so that we choose to reject and oppose God and His ways. Sin's only purpose is to destroy the life within us. The deceiver is the master of a disordered love, creating the affection for sin, abandoning the origin of love found in the true Creator known as God. Satan, the father of lies, is the one we serve when we accept and desire sin. S, for seeing. I, for inside. N, for nothing—seeing inside nothing. If the truth lives within us, we will see inside ourselves that sin has no value in this life or in the next. Sin is the affection for nothing. It is the affection for slavery, bondage, and the imprisonment of ourselves. It is the possessor of our heart, body, mind, and soul. It controls our thoughts and desires. And when it is part of us, it becomes routine or habit, part of our very being. It has deceived us and now it controls us. If by God's grace we come to the knowledge of it we might find we have a battle ahead of us. Sin is fast and very cunning. It pierces the body and enters the soul without the body's knowing. Our soul begins to hemorrhage towards eternal death, while our body delights in the sin itself. Body and soul: one vessel consumed by sin, drinking of the same fountain, tasting of the same tainted water with the sweet taste of honey, not knowing the poison hidden within it. Sin is pleasing to the flesh, but it contains the poison of eternal damnation, and the only antidote is the grace, mercy, and love of God. We must turn away from our affection for sin and hate it with all our heart. It is the only way. There is no reason to desire something that offers us nothing. Temporary pleasures are only temporary, holding no value when it comes to eternal life. How can a person, while truly desiring eternal life, truly desire sin that can lead to eternal damnation? He must love one and hate the other, or hate one for the love of the other. To hate sin should truly be the desire of an individual, knowing in our hearts that our desire for sin separates us from spousal union with Christ. All of us are sinners, but what makes the difference is our trying to be holy and in union with God. This should be the truest desire of the heart. If we desire to live a sinful life, it originates from our choices in life. Our choices should have been to try to know God and His ways. A blind man without a cane, walking on a road towards a cliff, can only blame himself when he falls off the cliff and dies because he did not carry the cane he thought he did not need. If a person chooses to reject what Holy Scriptures and the Church teach about sin, then he is no different than the blind man without a cane. We can try to reduce the effects of sin to nothing, believing in our hearts we have a free pass to Heaven.

We might think we are young and have a lifetime ahead of us. We might not believe in God, therefore, believing there is no punishment for sin. Whatever our reason is, always remember: a blind man should always carry a cane not knowing what lies on the road ahead of him.

 Fallen Angel

Where you began to fall and how you fell is a mystery. We know you as a fallen angel and try to understand where you went wrong. How is it that your seeing the most beautiful of all love could turn you against it? You, who were created out of love, turned against love, itself. What passed through your thoughts when you were constantly looking at and praising God? Did love burn within you with divine ecstasy? Did you think it was going to be a world of angels in harmony with God's heart? Then the day came when you were looking into God's eyes when He looked into the nothingness and created the universe. Did jealousy touch your heart, or were you unaffected? Did you wait patiently to see what God would do next? Then within the universe you saw the earth and you watched on as God's eyes began to focus on one point in the new creation. God continued, as you watched His creativity give life to the earth. You watched the land separate from the water through the twilight of the new heavens. You watched God bring forth vegetation in many varieties and sizes, bearing much fruit. You watched the sun give light to the earth which showed all of God's newest creations. And when the sun disappeared, you saw the darkness that hid the earth from your eyes. Did thoughts flood your mind when you looked into the darkness? Then God filled the earth with an abundance of living creatures that inhabited the sky, the land, and the waters. Did you begin to turn your face away from God and wonder what was next? Then God formed man and you saw someone that resembled angels. Did your thoughts turn away from God and focus on the man? You looked into the man's eyes and saw that he was filled with emotions and feelings. As you looked closer, you entered the thoughts of the man and saw the spirit of God within him. Something evil started to well up in you and you went to raise your voice against God in protest, but were unable. Jealousy and hate consumed you as it came rushing forth from somewhere within the new creation. You cursed God, and God cast you out of His sight into the netherworld along with all who thought like you. There you remain, cursing and hating God, waiting for the opportunity to destroy His beloved creature. Then God created a woman, and you entered the man's thoughts and saw he was well pleased and full of gratitude towards God for this beautiful creature. You saw the woman near the tree in the middle of the garden, knowing that if anyone ate of that fruit it would open the doorway of disobedience. You convinced the woman, Eve, to eat of it, and in turn she convinced Adam. Then their disobedience flooded the earth. You found a distorted joy in this. God, seeing the damage you caused His creatures, cursed you and sentenced you. He allowed you and mankind to freely roam the earth together, because together each of you took your turn in disobeying God. He will always cherish mankind because He put His spirit within them, which He created in the image of Himself. The hand of evil still dwells among us, but the blood of Christ continues to wash us in the battle for good against evil.

 Broken Cup

Oh my love, how my heart breaks when I see those who doubt in Your real presence at the consecration of Your Body and Blood. The eyes of the unknowing who attend Mass faithfully week after week, who look upon Your Sacred Body and Blood with disbelief in their hearts. They partake in receiving Your Body and consume it, but walk away from your precious Blood when it is offered to them for fear of contaminating their own physical bodies. Do they believe Your Blood is contaminated by the mouth of another? Do they walk away not knowing, not believing, and not understanding that Your Blood contains life-giving substance free from sin and disease poured out for the spiritually weak in desperate need of healing? It does not minimize Your suffering on the cross and its purpose, but opens the door through the sacrifice of Your Body, becoming the food and drink needed to give life to our broken physical and spiritual bodies. At the last supper, You gave both Your Body and Blood, the Bread of Your scourging and the Blood of Your sacrifice, not one in substitute for the other, but both, for the renewal of our body and soul. As the physical body hungers for food and drink, whereas food cannot satisfy thirst and drink cannot satisfy hunger, so it is with the Spiritual self which desires to be satisfied in its hunger and thirst for You. There are some foods that can satisfy the thirst of the physical body temporarily, but not permanently, leaving the body thirsty and feeling incomplete. Your body contains food and drink, and yet the soul that desires to satisfy its thirst completely desires to drink of Your Blood. Your Flesh is real food and Your Blood is real drink. How I would desire that Your Flesh could satisfy my thirst and make me feel complete, but it does not. I long to partake in Your Blood so that my thirst can be quenched by the Blood of Your sacrifice that now burns within my veins, flowing through my body and renewing me within. How I wish that my love for you could be satisfied here on this earth, but I know that it will only be satisfied when I see Your face. I know that Your Heart is broken by those who freely choose to reject what You said and did at the Last Supper. Those who, in their hearts, do not believe in the real presence of Your Body and Blood that has been sacrificed for all to receive in faith and love. They refuse to believe and partake in the ultimate gift that will remain with us until Your return at the end of time. In their blindness, they have rejected the truth of the Last Supper and the gift given to the disciples, and all of us, to receive as an everlasting and more permanent union in the sacrifice upon the cross. The cup was broken and the Blood was poured out upon this earth, establishing a new cup that contains the Blood of eternal life, shed for all, to be consumed by all, so that all can be renewed in Your Blood. Even though we will always thirst for Your Blood at the Mass, Your love will satisfy our thirst within until we can drink again and renew our love for You through the cup that contains Your love, Your spirit, and Your sacrifice for us. Lord, when I was hungry, You gave me food to eat. When I was thirsty, You gave me spiritual drink. Even though I thirst and hunger for more, I will be satisfied.

Blind

The Servant:

Am I blind, unable to see what is hidden within the depth of my soul? Is my love divided, torn between two lovers—the world and You? Do I desire the rich and abundant foods of Heaven, or will I remain eating the fleshly foods of this world? How can I find You; to what depth are You hidden from me? How can I be immersed in Your love? You have shown me grace, and shown me some of the mysteries of Your love in the miracles that I have experienced. I have rejoiced in and praised Your name for them. When and how will my eyes be open to see You, in the mysteries of You, hidden within Your abundant love? I have read Your words, written through the inspiration of Your saints and have stored this information in my intellect, and yet I still feel far from You. I have restored my original promises to You, hoping this time it is for the right reasons: not as a penance, but as an act of love; not to prove anything to You, but for love of You.

Our Lord:

When does a child become an adult? When does an adult become lost and need to return to the trusting simplicity of a child? What is hidden within you is the true desire of your heart. You must surrender your carnal passions and appetites that you hid deep within your heart, but which are not hidden from Me. You must crucify your earthly passions and desires. Let My love become inflamed within you and purify you because you desire to be purified. Look through the eyes that should focus on Heaven. Do not look through the eyes of earthly desires, but through the eyes of heavenly desire. I do not require sacrifices or mortifications of the body. Many have rebelled against these very things and find them distasteful because they do not know how to love. These very things are outward signs of a person's love and denial of his selfish nature. If you choose to do these things, I will look deep within your heart to see if they are done out of love for Me. If they are, I will find them pleasing to Me, because they are done out of love. I did not have to sacrifice My Son for love of you and the whole human race; I did it out of love. Humility opens many doors to the heavenly realm, allowing souls to receive the many graces I desire for them. Wisdom contains a fountain of inexhaustible understanding of My ways, allowing the soul to draw nearer to Me. Call upon My name in faith, and the power of your faith will answer and rebuke the very things in your journey. I have blessed you with many spiritual gifts. Always give praise and thanks for them; do not lower your understanding of them, but raise your understanding to them. Within them are My graces and love towards you.
If you desire mystical ascension, give up your inner desires and will to Me. The true lover does not give himself to many, but saves himself for his one true love. He gives his heart and body completely. He is unable to wander off or to set his eyes upon another, because no one else can satisfy his love. He remains madly in love with his love.

 Children of Disobedience

From the beginning of time, when I created man and woman, I placed My spirit within them, including moral law and free will. It did not encompass imprisonment by the nature of love, but allowed freedom because of love. Within the will and conscious mind, one can respond freely by discerning what is right and wrong. Within human nature, the will responds to what is pleasing to Me or what is pleasing to itself. Through that first act which denied love, came the fall of the first man and woman. In that act of disobedience, they freely chose the love of themselves and their own foolish desires over the love of obedience that leads to the doorways of eternal life. The first sin against the chance and the opportunity to choose love over disobedience. Through the first act of disobedience came the denial of love which denied life and brought forth the first death. Through the first death, which encompasses pain and suffering, the physical body embraced what could have been denied through the act of love. Because My love remains pure, it continues to pour out upon the sinful, showering upon them hope and salvation.

That which is uncorrupted will cleanse and purify that which is corrupted. Through sin came death. Because death dwelt among the living flesh, the spirit within continues to cry out to the heavens to be set free. Because darkness slowly consumes the light within the children of disobedience, I continue to send rays of light and hope, piercing the darkness for these rebellious and sinful children.

The first disobedience is no different than the continuing disobedience; they both deny the opportunity to accept and receive My unconditional love. False love deceives the knowledge of true love which is found in charity and humility. Pride replaces love with self-love, turning the person against themselves and Me, denying them an existence in the true joy and love that is found in Me, alone. The first fruit that contains life became death through the first act of disobedience.

The new fruit that I offered contains life—not by the denial of it, but in the acceptance of it. The obedient taste this fruit and begin to feel the benefits of it as they continue to consume it. The more they consume, the more they will restore life to their spiritual body. The disobedient rebel against the fruit of salvation, bringing upon themselves the denial of truth. They turn their faces away from the medicine found within the fruit which is their only cure, choosing sickness over health. They consume the many fruits that contain the poison of eternal damnation, finding their flavors desirable without concern of the outcome. Some poisons are more deadly than others and respond more quickly than others, but eventually the fruits of disobedience will lead to eternal death with no hope of salvation. There is only one hope, one choice, one tree, one fruit that you should choose. To which tree will you reach out?

 Struggle

How hard it is for souls in despair, thinking there is no hope, feeling lost and abandoned by their own world, hiding within their own misery, feeling that I have forsaken them, when they have forsaken Me! They walk on the path, not looking where they are going, and walking close to cliffs in the darkness of the night. They fail to see the light that is behind them, that is shining upon them, because they refuse to turn around and look. So how do they perceive struggles and what understanding do they form in their own minds? There are those struggles that are brought upon an individual because of a road or avenue chosen. People fail to look ahead, trusting in themselves and thinking and believing they can walk the road ahead without any help or guidance. Their free will interferes with their ability to reason and they rationalize the truth necessary for the journey. They are blind children who refuse to open their eyes and their minds to those who could help them. I also allow them to struggle for the purification of their soul because they are unable to see their own sins within themselves. They taste of the honey that appears to be sweet, but is disguised by the untruth hidden within the taste. They hold onto the memories of this sweet honey, not knowing that the real taste disguised inside is a mixture of sin and offenses against Me. I chastise them in the hope of awakening what is sleeping within their very being. What is hidden within them is the knowledge of Me and of the truth. The bittersweet becomes desirable to that soul, and the soul continues to journey forward, immersing itself more deeply into the darkness, becoming blinder to the light that remains behind: the light which calls them to turn back to avoid the road ahead of them which leads to destruction. The soul desires the will that is formed by the sweet honey of sin. If the soul, by My grace, awakens and sees its false desires, it will choose to let go of the memories of the honey it had desired. Many choose and refuse to let go completely of these memories which they hold dear to their hearts, thinking they will be unable to live without them. Therefore, I allow them to continue consuming this honey until they taste the true bitterness hidden within it. When they find it distasteful, they will go in search of something sweet to taste. It is then, and only then, that they are truly contrite and desire to accept the honey that I have set aside for them. They know in their hearts that this is the one true honey, sweeter than that which they consumed before. I wish no one would struggle, but sometimes find it necessary, knowing that they could misinterpret the true meaning of My ways. I allow them to struggle so that they can purify themselves. It is their free will and choices in life that cause them to struggle. They choose to pollute themselves—not by My will, but by their will—choosing sin over truth. Only those souls who embrace My will and let go of their own, will embrace their struggles for the love of Me. Their struggles will not be burdensome, but will be yoked with My suffering. My love will be their joy and their suffering will contain My love.

 False Gods

Upon the canvas of their paintings are images of the things they possess or wish to possess. There are many shapes and sizes to the objects painted on this canvas: none of which contain images of Me. The canvas they use is made of a material containing deception which they purchased from the servants of the evil one. The paints that are used on the canvas are mixed with the pleasures and the impurities of this world and contain solutions of sin. Their thoughts and desires paint an image that is pleasing to themselves and offensive to Me. False gods, false images, brushed on by the hand of the artist in their world of darkness. They worship their bodies and glorify their souls with the impurities of lustful thoughts: all kinds of abominations and offenses against themselves and against Me who breathed life into their bodies. Their desires are painted on the canvas with a material that is only temporary. In time, this canvas will crumble and become ashes upon an unholy ground, only to be swept up by the caregiver and thrown into the fire to be burned. The paints of sin will boil in the fire of excruciating suffering, unable to burn away, but boiled for all eternity. There is a canvas of hope that was painted many years ago that contains the image of My sacrificial Son. On this image, no impurities or imperfections are found. Flawless in design on a canvas that is indestructible and untouched by the forces of evil, it contains the image and the source to eternal life. Beware of the many pictures and images that were copied from this canvas. There are many who have painted their own images from the original image, but contain false hopes that will lead many astray from the true Me. I am one God, three persons in one God. There are no other gods that you can serve or worship. Their thoughts and desires create many false gods which are displeasing to Me. There are many false religions, false paintings on canvases, that will not hold up until the end of time. The painting of My Holy Church contains no imperfections. They are not found on the painting, but outside of it; not on the canvas, itself. Many have witnessed the holy ones of My Church, representatives of the Church, turn their faces from Me and toward the vain world, bringing shame to My Holy Church. A weak soul wanders in many places that it is forbidden to enter. Many dabble with images of the things they find in front of them. Without realizing as they continue, they open up their hearts and minds to the materialistic world—the vain world of empty promises. They open up the cans of self-love and the boxes of instant gratification and begin storing these in their houses of conceit and pride. They become dissatisfied easily, and continue collecting until their houses will hold no more. When the spirit of hope and salvation comes to their doors, they refuse to listen. They think they have everything they have ever needed and wanted. They become children of vanity and lust, living in a household of vanity and lust, eating and drinking the sins of this world. My servants have offered them heavenly food and drink, but they refuse to partake. They turn their faces away from the heavenly banquet, and eat at their tables of deprivation.

 Purgatory

The Servant:

Lord, there are many souls who appear to be living sinful lives. Some act ignorantly, blinded by their pride, but some of them have charitable hearts and are compassionate towards others. Still they refuse to listen to the many who want them to understand and know You. Where do you draw the line between Purgatory and Hell? What is purgatory? Help me to understand.

The Lord:

I search their hearts constantly and give each soul many graces which many refuse to accept. I wish that all should be saved and that none should perish. They are in Hell because they freely choose to be there. They knew My laws and precepts but refused to obey them. Do not be troubled, my son; let Me help you understand Purgatory. Do you remember when you fell in love? You embraced both the joys and pains of human love which contains emotional suffering. Purgatory is love being purified. The torment you feel in Purgatory is your inability to embrace Me, knowing that soon you will be able. It is not like physical love which has no securities or guarantees. Everyone has a guardian angel to help and assist them in their journey on earth and in Purgatory, not in Hell. Each individual should call upon their angel in life. Some refuse to believe or ask their angel for help. They will rely on their angels in Purgatory to console them. First, one must suffer physical death, then spiritual cleansing. Many do not believe in Purgatory and rely on the blood of My Son to save them. I did not have My Son shed His blood to be abused, but to purify and save. A soul is washed in His blood but is unable to achieve perfection in one's physical life—free from sin. Sin is death and I am life. Death cannot dwell in life. New life is resurrected through purification and death no longer has its sting. Death is removed and life is raised up—the sinful soul is cleansed. In Purgatory the soul does not suffer once, but twice for the sins they committed. The first suffering is the suffering of regrets. They see the sin they embraced in life that could have been avoided by choosing Me over the sin. The second suffering bears the pain and suffering of the sin they embraced. The flame of My love burns within the flames of Purgatory, purifying the soul through My pure love, the only love that can purify the sins of the souls in Purgatory. My fire purifies the soul from sin and My water washes the stains of sin, allowing the stains of sin to be removed from the soul. This is done through the purifying waters of My grace and mercy. My grace gives them refreshment and hope. My mercy gives them forgiveness and understanding of My purifying love. Thus the stains of the soul are cleansed, allowing the soul to ascend, no longer carrying the weight or stain of sins: purified light ascending and merging with a glorified body.

Traveling Souls

Souls travel in many places, wandering aimlessly through the woods of the unknown without My grace. They travel through the darkness on an endless path—the road to destruction. So where do they travel and how far will they go before realizing they are lost? They crawl on their legs of despair and false hopes, away from eternal life, blinded by their desires, and unable to see Me traveling with them to guide and help them on their journey. The hand of My province does not abandon souls, but constantly gives them graces and shows them My mercy. They appear to be all-knowing and proud. Blinded by their self-love and their need for instant gratification, they openly and freely reject My graces—graces poured out upon them like the waters of baptism now over a body that is shielded by the souls' inner desire, masking and clouding its vision. What do they find in the forest and how do they see what is there when they are walking in the darkness? They walk through the forest with eyes of darkness which allow them to see only the things that dwell in this world, unable to see the graces of light which surround them. These eyes perceive the vain world as the only thing that will bring them joy. As the sun—the light of My grace—rises and continues to shine, it cannot enter the forest which is formed by the trees of their false desires.

The stronger the desires become, the fuller the tree becomes. The tree grows in height and thickness and its leaves offer them cover which they think is protecting them, but only harms them as it shields them from My light. The eyes of each soul begin to close and their bodies slowly start to decay because they have freely chosen to dwell in the forest of darkness. They planted the trees of sin and watered them with their desires of self-love, fertilizing them with their offenses. All kinds of abominations exist in the soil of their hearts, nourishing and building the forest. It is so dense that My grace remains outside the forest, surrounding it with a light so bright that one would think it could penetrate their forest, but it does not. I do not force the light of My grace and mercy upon anyone; I allow each individual to surround themselves with what they freely choose in life.

Those who love Me plant beautiful flowers whose fragrance is beautiful and pleasing to Me. These flowers are planted in the soil of self-denial and sacrifice and are fertilized in their desire and love for Me. These beautiful flowers become the virtue growing in them through My grace and light which are constantly being poured out upon them and continue to water them. How beautiful their souls are with the many graces they receive, not as a reward, but as a gift they open with great gratitude and thanks! Without the light, nothing can survive or grow. It does not only provide light, but also provides warmth. This spiritual light contains grace and mercy—the warmth of My love which is poured out abundantly. Only through the acceptance of it will souls be able to reach the mystical ascension in a more perfect union with Me. Graces that are rejected and returned to Me as an unopened gift leave souls with less grace, causing them to descend away from Me. Those who continue to descend will reach the bottom and those who continue to ascend will reach Me.

Desert Storms

Through the waters of baptism they enter the plush green gardens which are free from sin, allowing them to experience in their souls the garden of Eden before the fall of mankind. Children, when baptized, are unaware of this beautiful gift when they receive the baptismal water, allowing them to be free from original sin. This is opposed to individuals who carry with them the sins they accumulated in their lives; they receive through the baptismal waters a pure soul, free from original sin and the sins that they had accumulated. In time, both will leave the plush green gardens and head towards the desert in search of new water to drink and food to eat. Individuals carry with them the memories of the food and drink they used to consume and sometimes find it hard to let go—they continue to desire what they should have left behind. Both young and old were baptized by the same Spirit and will enter the desert at different times with the same results if they do not remain in Me. So why do they leave the plush green gardens and journey to the desert? They are without complete understanding of My ways and enter the desert trying to survive on their own food and drink. They had received some spiritual food and drink through the sacraments, allowing them to begin the journey through the scorching sun and heat of the desert. While in the desert, they begin to experience spiritual dryness due to lack of the spiritual drink found in the well of the living water which is My Son. This is necessary for such a journey. Because they try to survive in the desert on the food and drink of their sinfulness, they quickly become dehydrated and begin to see mirages, heading for them in spiritual blindness. They begin to dig in the sands of sin, unable to find the things to satisfy their needs which at one time appeared to have satisfied them. They become even more dissatisfied and continue to dig deeper until they are unable to dig anymore. Being completely dehydrated and using the last drop of the living water, they fade away into the desert mirage. However, the faithful servants persevere because they continue to drink of the living water. The scorching sun of temptation beats upon their souls, and the dryness of the air does not affect them because they rely on living waters—the Word is within them. They continue to walk by faith, and I allow the desert's storms to beat upon them. They find refuge behind the rock which is the hope of salvation—eternal life. They wait for the storm to end and dust the sand from themselves. They feel refreshed, surviving the storms of temptation and the sands of sin, and continue journeying forward with caution and wisdom, ready to face the next storm that lies ahead. They drink of the living water, rejuvenating themselves within, knowing in their hearts it is the only way that they will be able to cross the desert and survive the desert storms of temptation and sin. They walk the desert with nothing but the sandals on their feet and the tunic that they wear, carrying no money with them. They walk in total trust in Me, knowing in their hearts I will provide the food and drink necessary for the journey: real food and real drink which will sustain them through the scorching sun of temptations and the desert sands of sins.

Dark Nights

This is a journey towards the perfection of a soul, and to the higher level of humility necessary for a deeper intimacy with Me. It borders on the world's idea of depression and the world of spiritual ascension through suffering. In the dark night of a soul, My light is still present within the soul. I allow the frailties of the flesh and the sins of the soul to eclipse the light of My love while suspending the soul in the appointed amount of time necessary to accomplish My will within the soul. This allows for a greater dependency upon me so that the soul is less dependent upon itself—a soul can fall into deception on its own. How often a soul forgets its own frailties and weaknesses by returning to its past lifestyle because of the memories stored within itself! They were forged through a lifetime of human weaknesses that had been built up within itself over a period of years. Sometimes it may take several eclipses—these are stains of imperfection—in order for the soul to unite with My will. This is necessary to reach the higher level of love of neighbor and for Me. An imperfect soul must always continue to strive to accomplish a higher level of perfection of its own soul, washing away the stains of imperfection through My grace. Sometimes it is blind to its own imperfection by the deception of sin whether mortal or venial. So why an eclipse of My light? When the soul came to know Me, it began to find the darkness repulsive and grew in hatred of the darkness and the pain sin caused it. This is a natural response of the soul that wishes to achieve a higher union with Me and not of the soul that exists through a distorted understanding of Me. When I speak of a distorted understanding of Me, I am speaking about the individual who exists in the world choosing not to know Me fully, or the individual who has been taught about Me through false prophets and has a false understanding of who I really am. The true soul is the one that truly desires total union with Me. It finds no joy outside of Me; it exists in the world trying its best to accomplish My will which is the salvation of souls. It feels the pain of emptiness when My light is not present and has a respectful fear of dwelling in the places of darkness. It knows in its heart that the Devil is nearby and that temptations will be assailing it soon. In that state, the soul desires only to dwell in the light because My light is truth which is peace and joy. This is why these dark nights are necessary. It is the only road that the soul can take to move from its imperfection and sinful ways to a higher level of perfection through the road of humility. It is a gift of love which can be misunderstood as a chastisement, and many souls have fallen away because they fail to understand My love's purification. A purified soul in a state of grace can do great things in My name; a weaker soul can accomplish things in My name, but cannot fulfill My plans for a more perfect state. This leaves the soul in a higher level of imperfection and results in a minimum union with Me. Dark nights are days covered by the clouds of imperfection and sins, for where I am there are no nights, only days filled with light and love.

 Perfection

The soul's desire for perfection must be true to its desire for holiness and not superficial. Beware of the remnants of pride which will prevent a soul from achieving a higher perfection and more perfect union with Me. So how does an imperfect soul achieve a higher perfection in a more perfect love? The soul must first come to the knowledge of its own imperfections and frailties through the road of deep humility before it can attempt the ascension to perfection. There are those individuals who think they are holy and even appear to be holy, and yet the desires of their hearts for material things are hidden—from themselves and from others who remain blind. Though the body and soul are one, they should rebel against each other in their desire to satisfy their needs. The body relies on its senses to satisfy its desires, while the soul that desires union with Me rebels and hates the desires of the body. This results in the mortification of the body in an attempt to overcome its foolish sensual yearning, as each wages war against the other, fighting for a victory to gain control. The soul must desire that which is perfect in order to overcome the desire of the body, which desires that which is imperfect. When I speak of imperfect, I am speaking of the desires of the flesh: The desire for imperfect love in order to satisfy its own needs and not to seek the salvation of the soul, whether in friendship, companionship, or love of neighbor. True love is the concern for your neighbor's salvation. It does not entertain the things that can cause harm to a neighbor's salvation. One must also choose to love that which is perfect, whose love is perfect, and stop desiring that which is imperfect. Why does one desire that which is imperfect? The inner desire of their soul is corrupted by many things. The flesh desires a perfect life with perfect things, through an imperfect thought, not knowing what is truly perfect. It sees beauty in that which is sinful, tastes that which appears to be sweet, and is consumed by the poison of eternal damnation of which My mercy is the only antidote. Blinded by its passions and desires for the things that satisfy its senses, it is unable to see past the obscurity with its soul's inner desire to know Me. My Mercy allows many to grow tired of these illusions and to desire something better in life, thereby beginning the search for Me. I allow these souls to find Me and to choose freely to renounce and hate the body's desire to satisfy its foolish sensuality. I search their hearts and help them with My grace if they are truly repentant and sincere in their desire to be holy. One by one, they must freely choose to let go of the things they love, knowing in their hearts it causes harm to their souls. Once stripped of these, and growing in the virtue of humility, they can begin the journey toward perfection. They will grow in true love of Me and of their neighbor. Growing in virtues through their love, they will continue to ascend to a more perfect love and union with Me. Although they cannot love perfectly, their love is perfected through Me, as My love pours out through them. No one can achieve a perfect union with Me while here on this earth. They can only reach full perfection through death as a soul departs from its body of imperfection and journeys towards the light of perfection and perfect love.

Predestination and the Will

There are those who believe that I can only know the outcome of a soul if a soul is predestined. This would omit free will. If the soul has free will, it would be impossible to know the outcome of the soul because of the many variables and possibilities which would arise from their choices. Some also believe free will causes chaos in the world of predestination. There are those who believe that a soul is predestined making them puppets. They also feel that it is pointless to help others come to Me because they consider themselves chosen by Me to be with Me in Paradise. Little do they know about the love I have for them and for all of mankind. Some believe they do not have free will because without My grace they are helpless, unable to overcome their weaknesses. They think My ways are unjust, but it is their thinking that is unjust to themselves. I search the depth of a soul and distribute My graces according to their inner desires. They also fail to understand that My existence is timeless and their earthly existence is in time. They do not understand the nature of My spirit. I am pure spirit and they are body and spirit. I am pure consciousness. Out of My love for them, I have placed My spirit in them by creating everyone in the image of Myself. They were not created as a physical image of Me because I do not have a physical body. I gave them a conscience, memory, and free will. My children, throughout history, and even today, continue to ask how I know the outcome of everything and everyone. I will give you a brief understanding because you cannot completely understand the infinite with a finite mind. When I gave you life, I placed your life in a timed world while I have remained outside of time as well as in time. Within the same moment in time, I watch your life pass before Me. Because there is no time where I am, you died when you were born, and yet you are living your life to the fullest hoping to achieve a good old age. Over time, I watch and guide you and pour out My graces upon you. You are not predestined, and continue to have free will, but your life has already passed before My eyes. In My existence, everything has already happened, including the end times. I am waiting for the end of the universe and the whole human race through time when all will come to completion; where there is no time. Let Me help you understand this better. A woman lives to an old age of one hundred with her memory completely intact. Though her body is old and fragile, she is able to pass through her memory—not in time, but when she existed in that time. She collects thoughts, and can recall memories, never leaving the time she is in. She does this through her consciousness which contains My spirit. She is unable to relive her life, but is able to access it through her memory. She knows the good and bad she has done and is unable to change it. However, she has clear knowledge of it. She was not predestined because she had free will. My spirit was with her, and in her, regardless of whether she chose to accept Me or not. I have witnessed from the beginning of creation to the end of creation allowing Me to see all and to know all. Time is of your world.

The spirit is infinite and the flesh is finite.

Rose Scarlet

My son, did you ever see a beautiful rose in the middle of nowhere? Were you ever curious enough to try to understand why the flower only lasts a season while the thorns of the bush remain? Or why sometimes the beauty of the rose is overlooked and never seen because of one's lack of interest or understanding of its beauty? To some it is just a flower of little value; to others it is a gift that represents love. There was a white rose, sent from heaven, that I will speak to you about so it is not a mystery to you anymore. In your journey, you have come to a greater understanding and love of the beauty of this rose that became scarlet. The petals of this rose were shed upon this earth and trampled. It is the only rose that contains the blood of everlasting life. It dwelt among the thorns of this world, nourished by the roots of suffering. This rose lived but a season and its beauty was seen by many. When it reached its full bloom, it was ransom for a world in need of a Savior. It was Rose Scarlet; it was My Son, Christ crucified. I am not here to speak to you about His suffering, passion, or the price He paid on the cross. That is the language of your Protestant brothers and sisters who constantly remind you of the debt paid in full, not realizing there is more to My Son's life than that. I also know that it troubles you because you do not hear much about My Son's sacrifice from many of your brothers and sisters whom you dearly love in the Catholic Church. Do not let this trouble you. Many have heard about the message of salvation and love which came from My Son's suffering on the cross. Protestant or Catholic individuals have reduced the truth in their own interpretation. They do not realize that their thoughts have become empty words. They have failed to understand and know the true meaning and depth of the Rose Scarlet. My son, this beautiful rose was fully man and fully God. He had the heart of a man in the flesh, and the heart of God in spirit, and His spirit is the Trinity. His emotions contained flesh and spirit, and His love was fully immersed in the Trinity. His thoughts contained the thoughts of the Heavenly Father. His will was My will, and His spirit was My spirit. Many struggle to understand the Trinity. It is the language of great scholars and theologians without answers. The Rose Scarlet is a simple word in a simple language; mankind has made it complex. Throughout history many have misinterpreted its meaning causing separation and dissension among their fellow Christian brothers and sisters. Many wars—innocent lives lost—and many false religions were created due to misunderstanding the Rose Scarlet. My Son was, and is, the Rose whose beauty was revealed to the world. Scarlet is the color of the Rose when His blood was shed for the world. The beauty of the Rose and the suffering of the Rose was one, and will always be one. The Rose's love and My love is one. My love is the beauty of the Rose. The Scarlet is My suffering by those who continue to reject My love. The thorns left behind are, and will always be, a reminder of the sins of the world. Christ Crucified, Rose Scarlet; different words, one meaning—My love.

 Thoughts

Your thoughts are not My thoughts, your ways are not My ways, and your language is not My language. There are those who, in their thinking, consider My Son a radical and a liberal. My Son's words are the fulfillment of My laws. Why does man try to categorize and apply earthly thoughts to heavenly existence? Man tries to apply his thinking to My ways. My ways do not conform to man's ways. Can human thoughts apply to something that is supernatural—pure spirit? Can you apply human reasoning to justify My Son's motives or actions? They are My motives and actions—one will. No, you cannot! Did they create the Heavens and the earth? They did not give life to the creatures that roam it. The heavenly realm contains pure thought and reasoning without explanation. The earthly realm needs to justify and explain everything. Their thoughts have become a dangerous vice crushing their ability to reason and know the truth, leaving behind distorted thoughts twisted by incorrect thinking. Applying human thoughts is an attempt to try to understand and explain the heavenly realm. Before one can begin to understand the heavenly realm, one must ascend to the highest mountain in the spiritual ascension towards Heaven. Most thoughts of an individual come from the top of the worldly mountains instead of the mountains of truth. Their thoughts come rushing down the mountain of worldliness taking My pure thoughts and clouding them, leaving a soul in confusion, unable to discern My will. Then they apply their thinking, corrupted by human error and judgment, which they believe to be true, and create a concept in hopes of explaining something that cannot be explained. My thoughts are a remedy when received by a soul in a state of grace and in a deep intimacy with Me, not influenced by the thinking of the world. This soul trusts totally in Me and has surrendered his/her soul to Mine. They have humbled themselves realizing how weak and frail they are without My graces. Children who are becoming wiser look towards Me for guidance. My thoughts now can flow through their soul's mind rushing through them like that of a heavenly rain washing down a hill towards the river banks. As spiritual rain continues down the mountain it increases in flow, gushing downward towards the ocean awaiting its arrival. The soul, being the open ocean, receives the heavenly waters with great joy and greater understanding of My will. Their thoughts and My thoughts are connected by the rushing waters of Heaven. They are not in need of answers, nor do they try to explain things that require no explanation. Their language is simple and their words are few. And when it comes to worldly matters they have no interest in them. The vain world is empty to them. They are constantly praying for the salvation of souls, hoping that My mercy will save them. Their thoughts are focused on Heaven, constantly seeking refuge in Me, not in inordinate love but heavenly love. Their thoughts are focused on My ways, and My ways become their thoughts. Their language is My language and their words My words. They become living mirrors reflecting My Son's love to a lost world.

Powers of this World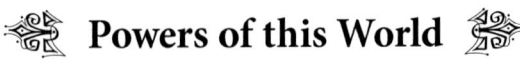

In your prayers you petitioned Me to intercede for a world in turmoil, as you call it. From the very beginning of time the human race was given free will and with their free will many changes came about. I created a world in a beautiful setting so that everyone could live in harmony with each other. I provided ways so that there was enough food for everyone. It began with one selfish heart influenced by the purest of evil and hate—the fall of mankind. It was not through the actions of the flesh, but the thoughts that entered the human mind. Satan wanted equality with Me and thus corrupted mankind to achieve the same. Satan's evil desires entered the world slowly through the root of evil and continues to flow into the minds of innocent individuals, creating desires outside of the inner desires which I placed within them. Instead they chose evil over good to satisfy their own selfish needs. They rejected the two greatest commandments, love of Me, and love of neighbor. My commandments no longer resonated in their hearts and souls. Sickness and disease entered this world via the broken nature of mankind. My love was the medicine to prevent all sicknesses but the world chose to reject it. Their bodies became corrupted by a disordered love, opening the floodgates to diseases and famine in the world. As they continued to grow in their disordered love, they continued to feed their bodies and souls with all kinds of impurities. Being impure vessels that could never be satisfied, they went out in search of more. They began to develop higher levels of disordered thinking and higher levels of disordered love trying to satisfy their flesh. The roots of disordered love inflamed their hearts, and My love was no longer enough to satisfy them. I let them go to themselves and their foolish sensuality. They turned on Me like Satan and all the other fallen angels, choosing the world of false powers and dreams over the heavenly realm. Evil spreads upon the earth like a mudslide down a mountain, destroying everything in its path and leaving behind the carnage of broken souls damned for eternity. Love of Me, their God, was replaced by love of self. They considered themselves their own god. Love of neighbor was replaced by love of self. True love was replaced with a false sense of love. Disillusioned, they no longer knew the truth and replaced it with a new truth. What was good is now distasteful, and what was evil is now desirable. That which was pure is considered offensive, and that which is impure, desirable. The seven deadly sins have replaced the virtues necessary in forming the conscience of a righteous individual. I have interceded for many, but fewer and fewer ask for My intercession nor believe in it. In holy scriptures My Son said that when He returns, will He find any faith? The powers and influence of evil in this world are strong, sin runs rampant, and the desires of the flesh are out of control. There is only one hope: My Son, Jesus. Let His words be the only words that resound in the hearts of mankind.

 Hidden

I am benevolent! How many believe this? Does anyone truly understand what is hidden within themselves? Are they capable of searching the depth of their own soul? You asked Me why certain individuals appear to excel in graces, while others struggle; are they really unable to advance to a deeper intimacy with Me? Always remember, My ways are a mystery! Many rely on their intellect for answers and through their intellect try to reason and rationalize who I am and who they are. I do not dwell in the intellect, but in the hearts of everyone. I know there are many who want to change who they are and feel abandoned because I do not answer their prayers. Their prayers come from their emotions, sometimes lacking the ability to reason. They misinterpret the trials and tribulations that come their way. I did not create anyone abnormal or want them to feel out of place. So why do I allow them to struggle in their sinful lifestyle? Their crosses are not a disorder in My design, but a grace to overcome adversity. Generations of sinfulness have corrupted and, at the same time, erased the memories of the truth. Over time, their sinful ways became a new way of life. What they wrote on the tablets of their hearts is etched in stone and must be broken. Would I distribute My graces upon an open body of water only to have them sink to the bottom with no one to receive them? So it is with a soul that does not know Me and chooses not to know Me. A soul that is truly contrite awaits the treasures of Heaven and becomes like a hole dug in the ground. It waits patiently to receive these heavenly graces. When I distribute My graces, they flow in search of a place to go, and finding the hole open they fall in and begin to fill the hole. There is not a shortage of graces. The problem lies within the human heart. The mind's intentions are not true with the inner depth of the heart's desire. Their senses continue to invite sin into their heart because they remain blind to it. Many say they want to be freed from something but they are only words resounding over and over in their mind. Within their heart is hidden their true desires, even from themselves, but not from Me. They cry out to Me, "free me, Lord, free me"! But in their heart they still want to taste the forbidden fruit, which I allow them to consume because that is what they want. Burned within their minds and hearts is the food of worldliness and their foolish sensuality, which they consumed all their life. There the battle begins, and My graces are the only thing that can free them from this bondage. They need to come to this understanding, but within them is a hidden formula of doubt. Their doubt takes away from My glory and the graces they could have received leaving them incomplete. They hide within themselves their own doubts and fears, exposing their lack of trust and faith in My graces leaving them helpless. It has been said that they cannot ask for My graces, without Me giving them the grace to ask for it. You might not verbally ask for My graces. But within your heart you ask for what might be hidden from your mind. I will search the heart of everyone looking beyond their words. There, within the depth of their soul, I find what was even hidden from them.

Impure

That which is sacred and holy in the supernatural will remain sacred and holy in the natural state through My Spirit that is contained within it. That which defiles comes from within the hearts of My people. They defile Me with their thoughts first, and then their bodies submit to their thoughts giving way to their sinful actions which is offensive to Me. Regardless of the state of their soul it does not change or alter My state or presence in the Eucharist. There are many outward and visible signs that are seen, but it does not determine what is within the hearts of those who appear to be holy. Many who appear to be holy tend to judge others when they should be judging themselves. What do they consider impure? Are their thoughts impure or corrupted by sin? Just as there are many ways to pray, is one way more reverent than the other? Is one less holy than the other? Also there are many ways to love your neighbor, as there are many ways to receive My love and graces. Do not become disheartened by the reception of My Body and Blood and how you are to receive it. Let them be discontented because they fail to understand the external reception, whether on the tongue or in the hand, because of tradition. They fail to understand that the external reception of My Body and Blood is not the greater value in comparison to the inward reception of Me. The heart that loves much receives My Body and Blood in a deeper, intimate way. It is not because they received it on the tongue or in the hand, but because they receive Me in a state of grace, worthily receiving Me in love. My apostle, St. Paul, speaks in holy Scriptures about receiving Me in a state of unworthiness. He does not speak of the external reception of Me but the inward reception. Those with great respect for My Body and Blood receive Me in love, and it is not a lack of respect for Me by the avenues of the physical body whether by tongue or hands. Everyone is a sinner with an impure soul who receives Me. They often forget that their tongue or hands have engaged impurely. It is the tongue that slanders and the hands that have failed to do My will. Both are guilty and unworthy of My Body and Blood touching any part of their body because of their unworthiness. I allow My Body and Blood to be received because neither one is capable of corrupting that which is pure by the avenues of the impure. My Church has suffered much, not through My spirit that is within it, but through the people within. In their own arrogance, they presumed to know everything, committing abominations against Me and My Holy Church. There are many churches and many denominations, and I love each and every one of My children wherever they might be. If each and every one of you only knew how to love one another in a greater capacity, then you would come together in a greater love of Me. Where does the truth exist? Each and every one of you claim to know the truth. Many make the claim that the Holy Spirit is guiding them, and yet they fail to see themselves for who they really are. I am the truth and the way; I am the resurrection of life; I am perfect and unending. The human race is not. Human error is real, and misinterpretations are dangerous. Seek humility and you will find Me.

 Go Back

My child, I know that you are apprehensive about where I am sending you. I know that you did not want to return back to the world, but wanted to remain secluded from it. You have many concerns about what will be expected from you. Do not let doubt and fear flood your soul. Trust Me, I will never abandon you. I wanted you to write a book not to shame or humiliate you or the people you love. No, I needed you to give a testimony to human weakness and frailty through your confession and your conversion. Many souls have plunged, and continue to plunge, into the world of darkness and are in great need of hope. Hope is the only vessel that can travel across the sea of darkness into the world of light. You continually ask Me why I did not choose someone else for this mission because you think you are inadequate, and that you will not be able to accomplish My will. Remember, without My grace, you and everyone else would be unable to accomplish anything in My name. My name and My will, is your strength, and through that you can accomplish anything, for nothing can defeat that. You are also stronger now than when you first converted. Although you are still a sinner, your love for Me is immense and that will be enough to carry you through your journey. I know you think that you continually let Me down because of your sinfulness. But in your deeper humility and your desire for humility, you will succeed. Your humility will be noticed by some individuals who appear to be worldly; that is good. Know that My eyes will notice you, too. Wipe away the tears from your face, those tears of gratitude and love. I know that you constantly remember how I saved you, and how much I love you; that is good. Sit and rest, catch your breath, let My love flood your soul. I know you have concerns about being rejected, laughed at, and being humiliated. I also know that you are strong enough to withstand what lies ahead for you. Your love for Me, along with your humility, is stronger than any fortress that was ever built by human hands. The world cannot take what has been built within your soul through the outpouring of My love and graces that were given to you. Even if your flesh should be fatally wounded or die, your love for Me will endure forever. The world no longer possesses your heart. That inner freedom that you feel is also your outer strength that will be revealed to those around you. You can go back with confidence and security in the One who sent you, knowing and trusting in Me. A sheep among wolves, or a mouse between two cats, it does not really matter. Let My love, that is everlasting, remain in your thoughts, and put your fears and doubts aside. Walk in faith, go back to the world you came from, and give testimony to the truth. Remain in prayer, seek refuge in the chapel of My love. Sail across the sea, walk along the shore, catch your breath, look for the path and follow it through the world of the unknown. Look at the footsteps of the many who walked the same path ahead of you. Feel their joys and sorrows, endure their sufferings and hardships, embrace the love that they have for Me. Go back and there you will find the person you left behind. That person is you.

 Murky Waters

In your continuing search for Me, you have climbed the mountains of joy, sailed across the oceans of hope, traveled through the deserts of despair, and now it is time to swim in the murky waters of your deepest sins. In this place the visibility is poor and the soul feels its most vulnerable. I have allowed you to experience an even deeper darkness of your soul which I know causes you much suffering. This is necessary for a sinner, who in their past, by their own choosing, chose a life of sin over Me. You ask Me why I am allowing you to experience this abandonment, as you call it. It is here that the remnants of your sins, that remain deep within your soul, begin to surface through the purgation process. As you grow in a deeper love of Me, the surface of your foolish, selfish sensuality begins to diminish. Below the surface are the sins that were covered deep within your soul. As the surface becomes uncovered, the deeper sins begin to draw closer to the surface and their roots start to break free from the loosened soil that once was solid by the weight of the sins above them. The loosened roots try to reach out and cling to something solid in an attempt not to be uprooted. As they are drawn closer to the surface, they draw themselves closer to the soul's eye. The uprooted sin becomes more desirable and causes great suffering against the new will. This is temporary; you need not feel abandoned. I have never, and never will, abandon anyone. It is they who abandon Me. The pain that you feel within is the result of your old, deep, uprooted sin battling against your new desire to please Me. Your old will is battling against your new will. Your love for sin rebels against your love to be cleansed and purified from sin. Your love of self rebels against your love of neighbor and Me. I did not remove My graces from you. The graces that you received are still within you. The uprooted sin is now closer to your intellect in the final battle towards the mystical ascension. The root that was deep below the surface is now closer to the surface, and now is a stumbling block. Now you must rely on the wisdom that I have given to you; it is your only hope. I am withholding any additional graces so that you may choose through your ability to reason and discern. In the dating process, you experienced the courtship. Now you must choose whether you wish to proceed forward towards the marriage vows or remain where you are. It is sometimes very difficult, when in murky waters, to choose a direction to go. It is here that one puts one's faith in what they have learned and have come to understand. It is here that the senses respond to the wisdom that is within. It is here that the senses are tamed and controlled by reasoning. It is here that you must choose the perfect will over the imperfect will. If you choose wisely, then your deepest, most inner desires of your flesh will be completely uprooted and burned through the fires of your burning love for Me. This new fire will consume you and purify you. The murky waters will evaporate around you. You will find that you are standing on the threshold to the depths of your humility, and you will see that I was with you the whole time.

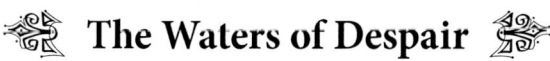 The Waters of Despair

My son, I know that you have experienced moments of despair, and this troubles you. Do not become disheartened. Everyone will experience the waters of despair at some point in their life. Some will continue to walk towards them, some will continue to step in and out of them, while others will drown in them. The waters of despair are not from Me, but are the deadly waters of the devil. Even the great Saints experienced the waters of despair. You ask Me, why do I allow this? If I did not allow this, free will would not exist, and you would be unable to choose hope. The greatest of love is built through faith and hope. It is there that it all begins. One must have faith in Me—the living God—and not put their trust in themselves. They must put their hope in the resurrection of life and believe wholeheartedly in it. Though charity and mercy are expressions of love which can be given from a believer or a nonbeliever, it does not define the greatest of love, which is I. Faith and hope now become the foundation for a spiritual house—pure love—not a house built by hands but by faith and hope. To avoid these waters, one must journey deep and far towards the mystical life; it is not an easy road. I have placed My spirit in every person; each and every one of you have the opportunity to grow in love and a deeper union with Me. Everyone has their trials and setbacks in life which are necessary for spiritual growth. It is how one perceives and accepts them, whether with an open heart or a rebellious heart. Weak or no faith leads a person to the waters of despair so often that they can hardly receive the waters of hope. They become discontented and turn against themselves and the world that surrounds them. They constantly bathe in the waters of despair until they drown, not realizing the waters of hope were right in front of them. Then there are those who have some faith. They are the ones who constantly go back-and-forth to the waters of despair. Before they know it they have formed a path and continue to go deeper until they are up to their necks. It is there that they cry out to Me, in times of need. I help them back towards the shoreline, and when they are satisfied they rely on their own strength and again begin to head back even deeper until they fall away and drown. Then there are those who are stronger in faith. They visit the waters of despair and spend little time there. They know they do not belong there but are unable to help themselves. They are the ones who begin to put their hope and trust in Me. They repent their doubts and turn away from the waters of despair and head towards the waters of hope. Then there are those who, over time, established great faith in Me and My ways. They are the ones who begin to walk towards the waters of despair and immediately stop and turn around because they refuse to doubt My ways. They have a greater understanding and trust in My providence. They live in My peace and experience the true joys of the waters of hope. Everyone must walk the path. They must choose between the waters of despair or the waters of living hope.

How do I Love You

I have never written any of my writings without feeling Your presence near me. Today I am writing to You from my heart, wishing I could feel Your presence near me. I do not know even where to begin. But I feel love is best expressed when you feel separated from the one you love. So how do I, who am just a mere human being, speak to a living God? How does an imperfect vessel, whose actions which are imperfect, show expressions of love to that which is perfect? Knowing that my words and actions might be some form of love that can never compare to Yours, how can I show You that I love You? I have fond memories of when You saved me from my wretched self, and even more memories when You carried me through the difficult transitions in my life. I also have memories of my ungratefulness towards an all-giving and loving God. I would consider myself an ungrateful child, but somehow You never let me feel that way. You opened my eyes to the truth, showing me that it would come at a price, albeit nothing in comparison to the price Your Son paid. You showed me great examples of Your love and continue to show me, and yet I wonder when I will truly understand. How blind will I remain before I can clearly understand and see that I may love You in the way You deserve to be loved? How many years have I loved You out of a servile fear? When will I experience You to the fullest—the deepest intimacy with Your heart? When will I choose to love You over the world completely, and not give the world another thought? You have sacrificed so much for me, and I wonder if I am blind or stupid.

Sometimes it makes no sense at all. At times I have chosen to love imperfect things over that which is perfect. Why do I choose sin and the deception of it when I should know better? I know that all of us have our fallen nature, but how many times can we use it as an excuse not to desire a deeper intimacy with You? I will find a way, with Your grace, Your mercy, and Your love, to the doorway of Your heart so that my heart can receive You without limitations or restrictions. I know that I fail to offer myself up completely to You, and I still rely on human consolation. Over the years, I have sown many seeds in the soil of my heart which have grown and flowered; not producing the fragrance of love but the odor of sin. Slowly, with the light of Your truth, these flowers of darkness will diminish. Yet I still feel far from You. I know that the odor of sin still mingles with the sweet fragrance of the light of Your truth, but Your truth is stronger, which brings hope to the garden of my heart. I will wait to hear Your voice that speaks within me from time to time, the sweet sound of Your love as it echoes in the chambers of my broken heart. I will strip my soul naked by removing the clutter of the filth that is within it, whether it was my sinfulness or my desires of this world in the hope that You will find its emptiness desirable. Let my body not offend You by its sinful actions. Let my eyes see only good, my ears hear only truth, my mouth speak words of comfort and love, my hands give You praise, and my feet always walk in Your direction. My words and my actions will never be enough. So let me give You my heart, someday a heart filled with Your love.

 Do You See the Evil

The eyes see evil differently than the heart because the eyes can only see the surface and try to comprehend through its intellect. It applies reasoning to the things that cannot be completely understood through the intellect. But then the heart is limited as well, because it responds through emotions. The depths of evil can only be seen and understood when a soul reaches the depth of humility through a deeper intimacy with Me. For many years you have asked Me, why do I allow evil to exist and prevail at certain times; especially when it comes to the martyrdom of My great saints? Where is My victory in such sacrifices?
Evil only appears to prevail in that moment of the sacrifice, but love prevails continuously through, and after, the sacrifice. My Son's love was never extinguished through the brutal suffering that He had to endure.
No, His love was elevated through what He suffered. My prophets, apostles, great saints, and martyrs were examples of My love, which was expressed through their sacrifice. Each and every one of them saw the evil, not just with their eyes but with eyes of their souls. They were able to see the sins within themselves and the evil in the sins, because they knew that I found them offensive. I am not talking about human emotions, but a clear knowledge and understanding of evil in the sins that dwelt within them and surrounded them. It was My grace that allowed them to see with a holy hatred the evil that could not be seen with the human eye or understood by the human intellect. Let Me give you an example. In this age, lust burns in the hearts of many people. What is seen through the eyes now floods the senses where it becomes an unquenchable fire that consumes the soul and leads to all kinds of sexual sin. Finding it pleasing to the flesh, the individual no longer has an understanding of the sinful nature of this invited guest. The soul is consumed with lust, and its senses become imprisoned because of the memory of those sinful acts. Now the body and soul is unable to free itself, nor does it have the desire to do so. Unfortunately, many will remain blinded, unable to see the evil that dwells within them and surrounds them. You yourself were blind for many years, even after your conversion, to some of the evil that dwelt within you and around you. You asked Me why you remain blind. Clouds cover the sun's rays, but when they dissipate the sun is seen in its full splendor. The clouds of sin took years to dissipate, and now it is time for you to see evil for what it really is.
This vision came with the rains of despair which I allowed. This mixture of rain and sun is the antidote which was necessary to despise that which is evil, and desire that which is virtuous. What was once desirable has now become hated. These desires are now seen as selfish. They were not visible to you before.
The fond memories of the sins became rewritten, and now are seen in the light of truth. The devil will continue to seduce your soul, but will be unsuccessful.
It is because you now despise what you used to desire. Through your sacrifices, your suffering, and your love for Me, you will remain victorious even if you should lose your life because of your love for Me.

 True Freedom

A soul's journey towards true freedom can only be accomplished through an understanding and detachment from its inner desires to satisfy its selfish nature. A soul is wretched and often blinded by its own wretchedness. True freedom is found in truth, in understanding what real truth is. In your journey, you have come to realize that the wealth of this world is fleeting and uncontrolled with no guarantees. Why are the many wealthy never content with their wealth? Why are they always searching, trying to acquire more, unable to satisfy their inner desires? They appear to be happy, but are unable to find true happiness because they are unable to possess true wealth which can only be found in Me. What treasure on this earth can ever compare to eternal life? What about the desire for power? You know now that the desire for power leaves a person feeling inadequate.

No one can ever possess enough earthly power to satisfy their inner desires to be great. They think that true power consists of controlling others and the circumstances around them. Yet, they are unable to control their own soul and its desires, leaving them out of control and powerless. They must humble themselves and seek the road to deeper humility because the proud live a lie, concerning themselves with what their neighbors possess and what the world thinks of them. When it comes to advice, they always have one ear open when they are speaking, and one ear closed when someone else wishes to share their thoughts. They are never free because they are always concerned about things that are unimportant.

Unfortunately, many souls are lost, and there are many things that imprison a soul, leaving it powerless and unable to be free. How can they expect to hold their heads up when they refuse to look towards Heaven for help? They are constantly looking down at the lesser without concern for the salvation of their soul. They have no desire to ask for My mercy, or to be forgiven. They imprison themselves in the visible and refuse to free themselves of the invisible. How can these prisoners ever feel or embrace true freedom? Can a person lost in the wilderness feel secure and at peace? Can they drink water in the middle of the desert while looking at a mirage? In the middle of the ocean can they see the shoreline? Can they feel secure in what is insecure? So where can they find true freedom? They will be unable to find true freedom within themselves unless they have freed themselves from their worldly desires and their fears of losing, in this world, what they truly do not possess. They must come to understand there are no guarantees in this life, nothing worth putting their security and hope in. Whatever it might be, whether possessions, success, and even their health, it can all be gone tomorrow. What they store in their barns might be lost to another. What treasures they buried in the ground might be unburied and stolen in the middle of the night. My love for them can never be taken away even if they choose to reject it. My mercy will endure forever even if they do not want it. True freedom is free for those who embrace the crosses of My love. They only have to let My love burn within their souls. Then they can feel the freedom that comes from true love.

 Trapdoors

So many souls are lost through the doors that swing open and then close behind them, leaving them unable to turn back, blinded by the mind's eye. As the mind's eye begins to open, the soul's eye starts to close. As the mind's eye continues to open, the soul's eye continues to close. Now being a victim of the deceiver, they begin to respond to their senses which allow them to feel pleasure. The first door being opened through their pleasure senses draws them through the door, thinking they are in control, not realizing that the tempter brought them there.

If they had only looked through the soul's eye, they never would have walked towards the first door. Being weak in faith and lacking understanding of Me left them vulnerable to the tempter and his deception. As they pass through each door that opens and closes they move further from Me. Relying on their own strength, they are unable to open the doors behind them and return to Me.

They continue to walk towards the darkness of deception. I allow an avenue that will open the doors behind them, one by one, and return to Me if they choose to do so. The avenue of confession is the only way of opening the doors behind them. Depending on how deep they have entered the devil's palace will determine the amount of suffering required to exit that place of misery. The mind's eye has great memory and retains much information that the senses have sent it.

The memory was not created to trap a soul in its own deception, but allow them to remember the joys of true love found in the truth. My Spirit is the truth and the way. Human reasoning is unable to save anyone when trapped inside the palace of deception. They must realize that unwanted grace drew them toward the door. Then curiosity brought them through the first set of doors, then the memory took over. If their memory continues to engage in its past thoughts, they will become a victim to their own self. They will remain in torment even though they call upon My name. They must choose wholeheartedly, wanting to be freed of the suffering they willingly chose through the mind's eye, ignoring the soul's eye. Sometimes, I allow them to be crushed by their own thoughts in the hope of drawing them closer to the virtue of humility. If they are unable to perceive what I am doing, they will choose to remain blind. They will be unable to free themselves, and may be lost forever. A humble soul eventually will be freed, but the soul must be patient, enduring the suffering for the love of Me. As gold is refined through the fires, so must they be refined through the fires of suffering. It is the only way.

I can open up all the trapdoors at once, or one at a time. This is determined by the soul's need for virtues, and how soon it acquires them. The soul should never allow itself to be put near, or in front of, any doors of temptation. The soul should close the mind's eye and look through the soul's eye, and the tempter will be unable to bring them to the door. The soul should stay put, allowing My graces to enter, and it will not have to worry about walking through the door and falling into deeper temptation. I am always present; even if a soul does not feel My presence. I am not found in the senses, but in the depth of one's soul.

And when a soul cries out to Me, do not cry from your thoughts, but from the depth of your soul, and I will hear you.

Descend to Ascend

This journey of suffering is necessary for you to personally undergo. It is the only way to open your eyes and humble you. You were blinded by your lack of true humility. You are still relying on your mind's eye. This can cause confusion in the decisions you make, and how you perceive them. You have seen many souls in their wretched state, and this has always troubled you since your conversion. You have seen what you consider evil and still fail to understand these misled children who are lost and abused and victims of sinful people. In your mind's eye you had some understanding of this, but in your soul's eye you still remain blind.

In your mind's eye, you knew that you should have prayed for these victims of unspeakable circumstances. You did not because your heart was still flooded with self-love blinding you to their suffering. I constantly had to crush you trying to humble you. The remnants of pride and self-love left you blinded, unable to love your neighbor as yourself. Now you have a greater understanding that one must descend in order to ascend. You were constantly crying out to Me thinking I was not listening to you. Then you realized that I, being the perfect Father, would not pick you up and hold you close to Me every time you cried out My name. Your parents did not when you cried out to them hoping not to spoil you. I, being your Heavenly Father—perfect love, knowing what was best for you, left you alone in your own despair and sinfulness. You saw this and how weak you were without My graces. You became more sensitive and understanding to those who struggle in their sinfulness. You hated your vulnerability and your sinfulness. You felt trapped and a prisoner of the devil and his manipulating powers. You were afraid you would never be able to defeat him. Then I gave you hope in your despair. You realized that I was pouring out more graces upon you. You finally realized how weak and frail the whole human race is without My graces. I allowed your soul's eye to descend to the depths of Hell and see My children on this earth as victims of evil. I am allowing you to ascend now because you have a greater understanding of the misery of these souls—innocent lambs being led to the slaughter. You now see them as victims of evil. Before you saw them as miserable sinners, which they are, but now you have compassion for them. I am more merciful because I love each and every one of you. If you wish to continue to ascend in your mystical journey, you will have to be My mercy and love. My great saints have inspired you. You desire to imitate them. They chose freely to become selfless and obedient to My will. My saints allowed Me to humble them and very seldom grumbled. I will continue to pour My graces upon you if you are willing to suffer more for the love of Me and My children. You feel like you have been through a lot already. That is only the beginning because I have to continue purifying you first. You must rely more on your soul's eye. Always remember patience will be the key to love. I will be your strength. You have come to hate the devil and all his lies. I have and will continue to be with you. The time has come to ascend and battle for the heavenly realm. You are a child of the light. Now leave the darkness behind.

Human Love

My son, it is My love that you must embrace wholeheartedly, letting go of your need for human affection—an insecure love. Human love is seasoned with imperfection, and it can cause much suffering to those who rely too much on it. I created mankind in the image of My love. The Ten Commandments are the foundation for true love. One should desire nothing else because in the end nothing else matters. Imperfect love desires imperfect things resulting in voids and empty pockets of temporal love. When I created mankind, I created them in a perfect love so they could love perfectly. Selfish love entered their hearts through the vessel of self-love and destroyed perfect love through sin. Sin pierced the soul through human thought. Imperfect love entered the mind, and at the same time perfect love was being emptied into the abyss of self-love. As you continue in your final search to satisfy your need for human love, you will realize that human love will never completely satisfy you. Last night I allowed you to see in your dream your father living in an apartment as if he were separated from your mother. You also saw on his bureau photographs of when he was in the service. As you began to look through his photographs, it brought tears to your eyes because you felt an emptiness. Meanwhile, your brother, who was in the room with you began to badger you with a sarcasm in his voice. This also troubled you because you felt he was insensitive to your tears. Your human emotions brought you to a bad place—the place of despair. Your father and mother are still together, but like any couple you saw there are moments in life that seem incomplete thus holding the key to unfinished love which is found in imperfect love. Human love is like the salt of the earth. When it loses its taste, it seems less desirable. Human love contains impurities which makes it impossible to achieve perfection. One can never feel complete through the incomplete. I sometimes pour graces into human emotions in the hope that an individual would return to Me. You personally have been graced through your suffering. You realize that human love can only satisfy you at certain moments in time. You are continually searching for the higher level of love found in the perfect love—My love. My love and mercy cannot be contained or bound, though it can be rejected. It still remains perfect and can be received perfectly through an imperfect vessel. The vessel of imperfection that is open to My love continues to be diluted by perfect love, becoming cleansed and purified, leaving it with less impurities. The soul that was filled with imperfection, now being filled with a more perfect love, is capable of feeling more complete and does not rely on human love to satisfy its inner desires to be loved. Selfish love diminishes, and the soul now being filled with sacrificial love, loves greater and no longer desires human affection to feel complete. Being totally immersed in My love, it appears to ascend towards Heaven intoxicated by the pure love that floods its soul. Being intoxicated, the soul now desires that all should experience the rewards of Heaven and live solely for the salvation of souls. Human love is a plank across a brook, My love is a bridge across an ocean.

Crucify the Flesh

The greatest accomplishment that can be achieved by a soul is the crucifying of its own flesh. You have been told by your spiritual directors that I want you to enjoy life here on this earth, whether through recreational or personal pleasures. They gave you this advice because their love for Me has become lukewarm. They have walked down the corridor of self-love too often and turned their backs away from the corridor of selfless love. I tell you that you will never achieve a higher spiritual ascension through worldly advice, or living a worldly lifestyle. You are to remain obedient to your spiritual directors in spiritual matters concerning the well-being of your soul, disregarding matters in the partaking of worldly illusions.

I will allow you to experience these illusions less frequently as you continue praying for a deeper and more meaningful relationship with Me. I love all My servants equally, but they are becoming more worldly, losing sight of their calling as they continue to fulfill the desires of their flesh. Some have brought shame by disgracing My holy church with their sinful desires. You must continue to pray for them and be as obedient to them as best you can without compromising your true call and the desire of your heart—a deeper and more meaningful relationship with Me. You have already begun to experience the suffering that comes with the denial of your fleshly desires through the avenue of fasting. Your flesh is rebelling against your soul's desire as it continues to torment you through the avenue of hunger. You have experienced some weaknesses, but remain persistent. You also understand the necessity of this suffering. Humility in the fires of persecution will also help you in your journey as you continue to crucify your flesh. Pride in any shape or form comes from the flesh and will continue feeding the flesh in small doses. You must annihilate any pride, whether hidden or revealed to the human eye. You must labor unceasingly always occupying your mind and body for the glory of Me. Many feel that comfort is something that they are entitled to, but I tell you that My great saints did not know comfort nor did their bodies engage in it. They labored unceasingly for the salvation of souls putting their own desires aside, and if there were any, they placed them in the flames of My love. They abandoned themselves and became orphans to the world. Their life was poured out like a libation in the pool of sacrificial love. The pleasures of Heaven were found here on this earth in the crucifying of their flesh. Their soul ascended taking complete control of the body and living totally in My spirit. They were outside the body's desires yet living within the body. The bitter taste of the suffering once experienced by their body became the sweet taste of Heaven within the soul. Suffering became joy with a new sweeter taste. The aroma of suffering was breathed in deeply, whereas before they hesitated and feared breathing it in. My graces flooded their soul, they became inebriated and became intoxicated with My love. Self love dried up and was swept away by the winds of denial. The crucified flesh hung helplessly under the control of the once imprisoned soul.

Heaven

Many have tried, and will try to understand Heaven. They are unable to understand this paradise. In the Bible certain prophets try to describe Heaven using forms of measurements such as cubits or foods to feast such as milk or honey. "Gateways through to Heaven's doors" were words used in an attempt to describe the heavenly banquet and the vast beauty and size of Heaven. Father Abraham talks about a chasm that separates. It is a chasm that separates Heaven from Hell—a chasm that separates My love from the world of hate. These were also written in an attempt to give some kind of description about a place that cannot be described. So what is Heaven? How does one describe a place without using metaphorical language or dimension? Let us start with the human body. The body and soul is in a union in harmony within itself, not body-soul dualism. Although the body is limited by its physical strength, the conscience—as the world calls it—the soul can search without limits. The mind is limited by the knowledge and understanding within it, but the thought process is not limited. The soul and the conscience are one, and the body and conscience are one.

How hard it is for the human mind to understand Heaven or Paradise.

Heaven and My love are one.

You ask Me, how can a place and emotions be one? How is the body and the soul one? The body works in the physical controlled by the mind—the soul. Can the body tell the soul how to respond? No, of course not. So it is with Heaven and My love. It was My love that created the Heavens and the earth in creation.

The body and the universe, which is part of My creation, were created out of My unconditional love. My love is found in the soul and can be expressed through the human body not vice versa. The human soul is capable of great love, in a pool of grace. What forms the conscience? It is free will for it chooses to live a lie or live in the truth. The flesh is limited. Heaven has no limitation, nor does My love have limits in the human soul. I limit and distribute My graces as I see fit. The physical body and the universe have limitations. It may sound complex to you, but it is rather simple. The human race was created in My image. My words were breathed upon My chosen ones who wrote the Bible. Their words are My words, and yet we are very much separate. No one can ever face Me in sin—impure love.

I am pure love that constantly watches over them and is part of them. My spirit dwells in them and dwells in everyone. I have no physical form and yet I took physical form in My son Jesus, and yet I remained in Heaven. My love took the form of flesh as well as partaking in creation—I love all creation. I created everything through My love. My love exists in everything that is good.

You call Heaven a place as everyone else did before you, but I tell you Heaven is My love with no end or dimensions but a complete immersion into My love and very much part of Me. The levels of love or intimacy are felt as one is drawn closer to My innermost Spirit, like one who draws closer to the sun's rays.

I am not a place in time or space but am all-knowing. I exist beyond the human race's greatest understanding of love.

I am Heaven. It will be found in Me—My love.

Imperfect Lover

My son, you are unable to know or understand how much I love you and all of My children. The human mind does not have the capacity to understand perfect love. It is unfathomable to the imperfect lover. (You ask Me, how does My perfect love, love such imperfect lovers?) It is because perfect love can achieve the impossible. Human love cannot love perfectly because it does not understand or have the desire to love perfectly—flawed by original sin. Perfect love is full of compassion, mercy and justice. Perfect love is not corrupted by sin or human emotions. It is unaltered, unchanging and unmoving. Human love is like a prostitute who gives himself/herself away without a thought of offending others, seeking his or her own earthly pleasures and needs. At times they give Me lip service and announce to the world how much they love Me. They are like the Pharisees and Scribes. They give themselves away to their senses and emotions, bathing in their sins unable to smell the stench around them. Constantly trying to satisfy their passions and desires, they are like a boat being tossed across the ocean by the gusty winds and stormy seas. They try to sail across the ocean without directions or understanding, entering unnavigable waters thinking that they are alone with all the answers. They love imperfectly because they refuse to embrace My perfect love fully. Everyone is flawed; they can never love perfectly because the remnants of selfishness remain within them. Some are more selfish than others. Some would choose to go down with the ship before they call upon My name; choosing to drown in their sin instead of being saved. Others will abandon the ship hoping to stay afloat on some of the wreckage hoping to be saved, but will return to their lifestyle again. Others will never board the ship having the wisdom not to enter unnavigable waters alone. My children will always remain imperfect lovers, but they should never give up hope. Although you are imperfect, you still can love much and do great things in My name. Imperfection seasoned with humility can sweeten the taste of love. My grace can inflame love allowing it to burn stronger and brighter. Sacrifice can strengthen the endurance and capacity to love. Mercy can strip away self-love purifying the imperfect lover. Forgiveness can tear down the walls of pride allowing love to sweep across the floors of hate. Prayer strengthens the soul allowing the soul to enter into a deeper, stronger, perfect love. Fasting mortifies the body by denying the senses. This allows the imperfect lover to embrace the suffering that is necessary to understand denial. You were created to love and in doing so means your life must be poured out as an offering for the salvation of the world. Your imperfect love still can do great things because it contains a mixture of My love and grace. Throughout history My love was poured out through many, and many have been saved through the imperfect lover. Now those imperfect lovers have entered Heaven and now live in perfect love. Always remember that those imperfect lovers in the moment of love have loved perfectly because in that moment My love passed through them. Thus, they received a taste of Heaven and a taste of pure love.

The Pool

There are many who refuse to enter the pool of My love and mercy fed by the springs of eternal salvation and hope. The waters are clear, bubbling up with My love and graces. The waters contain no deception as they are filtered by the sands of truth. There is no bottom allowing the soul to swim as deep as it desires. A soul can swim in an endless reservoir of saving grace. These waters are refreshing and life-giving, unable to be polluted by the sins of the faithful. The world's deceptions cannot enter these waters because they are, and will continue to be filtered by My truth. As souls continue to bath in these waters, they draw more of the living water into their souls, filtering out the sins within them that were drawn from the pool of eternal damnation. Some of their sins head towards the sidewalls and are filtered through the sands of My truth unable to return to them. Other sins begin to dissipate and evaporate. This pool of water becomes more life-giving and refreshing. The soul becomes lighter and freer and begins to ascend to the surface towards the light of My love. They become more inebriated by the waters of truth and inflamed by the rays of My love. Once cleansed they become imitators of My son, carrying out the good works of love. They share My mercy, love, and My truth to a world in desperate need of salvation. So why do so many stand outside this pool which is readily available to everyone? Some choose to stand outside looking at the pool afraid to enter because it means that they will have to give up the lifestyle they are living for something less pleasing to the flesh. Others choose to test the water on occasion when convenient for them. They splash the water around waiting for something special to happen immediately, because they live a lifestyle of instant gratification. Others approach the water when they are in need of help or want prayers answered, and when they receive no response they turn and walk away dissatisfied. Others refused to enter the pool because of deception. The devil has convinced them that they do not need this pool because it is filled with a history of hypocrisy and lies. Others think it is a mirage, part of someone's imagination, man-made, so they continue living their life in their man-made mirage. To many the water seems obscure and unclear. Sin clouds their vision and they refuse to enter, wanting nothing to do with My love. They search the world for happiness in the waters of deception. They bathe in the pool of deception relying on their senses. The pool of deception has a bottom that continues to be filled with the stones of deception and lies that fall from the walls of this pool. The vines of sins head upward from the stone located on the sidewalls towards the victim as they continue to bathe in this pool of lies and false hopes. Eventually, these vines begin to wrap around the victim. The victim becomes entangled, unable to get out. The stones become loosened and begin to fall towards the bottom as they continue to draw from the victim's soul the weight of the sins contained within. The body can no longer stay afloat and is drawn to the bottom of eternal damnation entangled by the vines of sin.

The Final Battle

There are many who will never have to face this battle. It is the devil's last and final attempt to snatch a soul from Me. He will use all his wits and lies to deceive your soul, offering you worldly pleasures beyond your imagination, or he will try to enter your thoughts trying to create confusion. He has no concerns about the ones he already owns just the ones that have chosen to draw closer to Me. The ones who sacrifice much of themselves and their worldly desires to live a holy life, are the ones tormented by the devil. They battle temptations, mortify the flesh, crucify their passions and endure physical pain for love of Me. The worldly look at them and are unable to understand them, considering them foolish individuals. My holy ones are filled with My grace and love and often intimidate the worldly by their holiness. The devil is persistent and constantly attacking them. It may be on your deathbed where you might face your final battle when you are most vulnerable and weakened by the world that you will have to battle for My name. It is there the flesh will battle the spirit for the final victory. It will be there you might face your greatest moment under the torment of the devil. It is then that the flesh that you deprived yourself of will try to cry out for its last taste of this world seducing your mind in hopes of distracting you. With holy fire you can deprive and burn the last stronghold of the flesh. Your final battle will be fought when your worldly passions have been crucified by the spirit of My love. The desires of your heart will have established complete union with Me in the will. The battle will be in spirit not in your flesh for it is the devil that attacks by means of the flesh. All detachments will be accomplished, and your desires will be tested but not awakened. They will remain in a dormant sleep never to be called upon again by you. They will be dead to you and no longer will have control over you. My desires will be your desires, and your will will connect with Me in spirit not in your flesh. The devil will seduce your mind and body in many ways trying to break your will. Leave no crack for him to enter and give no space for him to breathe in the recess of your soul. He will try to create doubt and fear within you. Rely on My mercy and love to save you. Do not forfeit the wisdom that I bestowed on you; it will be part of your armor. Your shield will be My truth that dwells within you. There is nothing he can offer you that can compare to the rewards of Heaven. Flee his assaults and do not turn back as with Lot's wife who was turned to salt. It was her punishment for disobedience, and turning towards that which was sinful and desirable even when it was being destroyed, holding on to nothing, a fool trying to savor her last taste of evil over the good. That is where the devil gains his victory over the human mind and soul. It is in that last stronghold of the human hand grasping everything in his/her grip hoping to take the fool's gold to the next world of a make-believe paradise. It is the giving up of a life of eternal joy to spend a life with the damned in Hell. Victory awaits you when your hour will come. The attacks will be brief. Your suffering will be the tokens used to enter Heaven's gates, a small price for eternal love.

Illusions

One must try one's hardest to discern what is real and what is an illusion. What one might consider to be real or the truth can really be an illusion, formed through deception clouding one's mind, creating a false image of oneself and others. How do the worldly perceive Me? Do they know or understand that I am a loving Father who is merciful and compassionate, who understands them better than they understand themselves? I am everything they would ever need or desire, the perfect friend and perfect lover. Why is your love divided at times, and why are you blinded in those moments? You are not alone, for there are countless numbers of people who live in this illusion too. I will tell you why. Everyone has the opportunity to draw nearer to Me. I am available through different avenues. I do not use the same avenues for each individual. Each individual contains within themselves different flaws and failures, choosing to remain blinded to them. They are not willing to open their eyes forming their own opinion of Me. Part of the equation is the balancing of their spiritual and flesh desires to meet their comfort zone. They justify their actions by examining an individual worse than themselves and making comparisons on an unbalanced scale. Unholy are they who praise My name with a false heart, living in the flesh and pretending to proclaim in the spirit. I spent many years working with you in many ways to help you see past your own illusions. I allowed you to journey to your past with clearer eyes, seeing the pain you caused others and the many tears that were shed for love of you because of your selfish and arrogant ways. You were blinded to your self as well. I showed you the power of My grace. If it were not for My grace, where would you be today? I taught you humility and the power to crucify your passions. Now you feel the freedom and no longer feel imprisoned by your desires. I poured out My mercy and love so you could fly on angel wings and soar high above the world below that held you down. I also allowed you to drown in your sins so you could see how helpless you are without My grace. You finally opened your heart wide and realized I was a teacher, friend, lover, and father to you. You wanted Me to be proud of you like a son. There were many illusions that kept you from seeing yourself. One by one I showed you the errors of your ways. I taught you patience as I have been patient with you. My love bears your sins upon My shoulders as you continue heaping them upon Me. You lived in your world of illusions blinded by your pride. Your eyes are opening wider, and I am becoming more real to you. Step-by-step, cross by cross, drop by drop, you will walk, and you will shed illusion after illusion until you know the complete truth. I am the truth and the way. He who truly believes in Me will never die. Continue to come to Me. You have come a long way. I have held your hand when we walked the seashore and carried you at times across rocky grounds. I have given you a bridge to walk across, My son. The scales are gone from your eyes now. No more illusions. Go out to the world. Let yourself go and share My love.

Temptations

You have asked Me, why do I allow temptation, because it saddens you when you fall into them? Try to remember that every temptation one yields to is a victory in the eyes of the Devil, and a scourging to My Son. Falling to temptation increases the weight of His suffering—sins of past, present, and future. Many believe that My Son paid the price on the cross for their sins, rightfully so.

He willingly accepted the heavy burden of their sins that were heaped upon His shoulders at Calvary. His death was the ransom for the salvation of many.

It does not give you or anyone else the right to accept mediocrity when faced with temptation, or to make excuses for not fasting or offering sacrifices necessary for future temptations. What many fail to understand is the continuing suffering that pierces My Son's heart. The shadows of blindness remain in the world. Temptation that lead one to sin has lost its value in the hearts of many. All the offenses in the world pierce My Son's heart, causing the blood from His heart to pour out drops of mercy over a sinful world. His pain intensifies His love in a dual suffering.

The intensifying of His love creates a greater need for His mercy. The first suffering was on the cross. The second suffering is the continuing pain by the rejection He endures when a soul that is tempted falls, rejecting His love. Many are blinded to the reality of temptation, passing it off as human nature, thus satisfying their sinful desires. Others understand there will always be temptations and succumb to them anyway, because they feel too weak to battle them. The real blindness of temptation is the ignorance of not knowing the way out of them.

Wisdom is a grace given to those who continue in their search for Me. As they continue in their search, they enter deeper into My love and become more immersed in it. Grace abounds, and the soul continues plunging deeper into an unending pool of mercy and love. Temptations give the soul an opportunity to be courageous and victorious against the Devil. Here love is tested whether for Me or neighbor. Love that is proven through the purification and the suffering endured by the temptation now has great strength when seen through the eyes of truth. Now when the eyes of temptation fall upon a soul, the soul is purified by My love.

The soul sees the horrors and lies of the temptation and thus rejects wholeheartedly the pleasures and satisfaction offered within the sin, overcoming the temptation and avoiding the sin. The selfish pleasures that were rejected had no victory over the soul. True love abounds as selflessness excels and casts out the beast and throws him aside for the moment. The beast, being rejected by the servant of God, becomes infuriated as Heaven claims victory in the battle. The soul chose love over self-love. The Devil will return with an even greater temptation; waiting for the moment when the soul is most vulnerable.

He is waiting patiently to claim his victory when a soul falls. He claims his victory with a grin on his face while teardrops fall from Heaven. If one could only understand that every temptation is a victory or defeat, seen by Heaven and Hell. Every temptation has the capacity to bring joy or pain. There is great joy in Heaven when it is rejected. Great pain when one succumbs to it. What will you bring to Heaven's doors the next time you are tempted?

 The Heart of God

On the day that My Son died on the cross, His heart was pierced and out came the outpouring of His love. My heart, as well as the Holy Spirit's, was pierced too resulting in an unending outpouring of mercy and love upon the earth. We are three persons, one in unconditional love. Now let Us speak to you in the singular through this love. My love flooded the earth encompassing past, present, and future. This was the greatest outpouring of My mercy and love given to the human race. My love swept across the earth through time entering past, present, and future, entering the souls of those who desired My love and passing by the hearts of the flesh that refused to welcome it. The spirit of My love continues in a relentless search until the appointed time. I allowed My spirit to penetrate many hearts with the seed of My love. It took root in them and the seed of My love began to grow stronger. They worked hard on shedding their selfish desires in the hope of destroying the roots of self-love within them. They grew in size and strength becoming the plants of sacrifice and mortification. My graces continue to water them, and these flowers soon began emitting the sweet fragrance of heavenly love. They understood My spirit and desire wholeheartedly to leave the world behind them. They saw that many gave their heart to the world, and this saddened them. They saw the pain that the world causes Me with their sinful desires and actions, the world I created out of My love. They learned that true love is found in My spirit—pure love. They know that I love a humble heart that practices sacrificial love, so they chose to reject superficial love. They understand that My love is unending and constantly flowing, and it is just in mercy, and fair in the distribution of graces. Human reasoning cannot understand these souls that live in My spirit, and how they are capable of loving supernaturally beyond human capacity. It is because they do not rely on their senses that constantly indulge in the tastes of the flesh. They live their life by supernatural desire. This is accomplished when they experience My heart through the avenues of sacrificial love on their road to humility through great suffering. Few are willing to walk without grumbling. A discontented heart is unable to experience the joy found in Me because their heart does not belong to Me, but still remains in the hands of the world. They are blinded to My love which shimmers greater than any gem found on the earth and purer than any refined gold. No one can fully engage My heart because of human brokenness—the impurities found in human love. I allow them to immerse in My love and excel beyond human love which is necessary to bring souls to Me. Only with My love is the human heart able to accomplish My will. My love is capable of carrying their heavy burdens allowing them to endure great physical pain and emotional suffering. My yoke is light making the impossible, possible. Human suffering has no power over My heart. So let your heart go and be free of the suffering that possesses it. Unite it with mine and turn your sufferings to joy. It will be like two hearts beating as one and flowing as one spirit. It will be the true spirit of unending love.